Benefits Realisation

Benefits Realisation

The Change-Driven Approach to Project Success

Rasmus Rytter

WILEY

This edition first published 2022.

Registered office

John Wiley & Sons, Inc., 111 River Street, Hoboken, NJ 07030, USA

John Wiley & Sons Ltd, The Atrium, Southern Gate, Chichester, West Sussex, PO19 8SQ, United Kingdom

Editorial Office

John Wiley & Sons Ltd, The Atrium, Southern Gate, Chichester, West Sussex, PO19 8SQ, United Kingdom

For details of our global editorial offices, customer services, and more information about Wiley products visit us at www.wiley.com.

Wiley also publishes its books in a variety of electronic formats and by print-on-demand. Some content that appears in standard print versions of this book may not be available in other formats.

Library of Congress Cataloging-in-Publication Data is Available:

ISBN 9781119859789 (Hardback)
ISBN 9781119859796 (ePub)
ISBN 9781119859802 (ePDF)

Cover Design: Wiley
Cover Images: © aleksandarvelasevic/Getty Images
Printed and bound by CPI Group (UK) Ltd, Croydon, CR0 4YY

C9781119859789_050422

Contents

Preface

Every day, I get to work with something I genuinely love. My passion is to enable companies and public organisations to realise the full benefit potential of their business change projects. It is my hope that this book will inspire people to create the change needed to increase the value of the investments put into business change projects.

The purpose of the book is twofold:

- To provide a practical and case-based guide on how to get more value out of your business change projects.
- To make the benefit realisation method an integral part of your way of working with business change projects.

In 2015, I authored a book in Danish called *Gevinstrealisering* (*Benefits Realisation*) with my good colleague Jesper Krøyer Lind and Per Svejvig from Aarhus University. Together we defined what would prove to be a great stepping stone for the benefits realisation method, namely the benefit map. Since then, the way we use the benefit map has been refined and expanded to cover all parts of the project lifecycle. Furthermore, it has been adapted to accommodate new delivery methods such as SAFe (scaled agile framework). During this time, it became clear that if we wanted to realise the full benefit potential of business change projects we would need the same type of practical and hands-on approach to behavioural change as we had developed for benefits realisation. Succeeding with behavioural change is the key driver for benefits realisation, and too often we saw the work we put into defining and following up on benefits was in vain, as we did not succeed in changing our colleagues' ways of working, hence the benefits realisation method had to include a practical approach to behavioural change.

To really create value within organisations, it is not enough to apply the benefits realisation method on one or two projects. It needs to be used on every single business change project in the portfolio.

With the help of Jesper Krøyer Lind and colleagues from Implement Consulting Group, since 2015 I have gained a great deal of experience on the implementation of the benefits realisation method. While there is no one way to implement the benefits realisation method, the most successful implementations share a set of common features I will share with you in this book.

If you are responsible for realising the benefits of a business change project, either as a project manager or as a person with managerial responsibility, this book should be on your reading list. If you are looking for inspiration on how to create more value in your business change projects and increase your organisation's competitiveness and efficiency, this book is highly recommended for you. Read on and be inspired to design a project organisation that will create value no matter the delivery method.

Writing this book, I set out to make it as useful and practical as possible, ensuring that the content would be easy to understand and apply in the real world. I have therefore chosen to limit the number of tools and approaches for working with benefits and change. This also means that a lot of tools and recommendations for ways of working with benefits and change did not make it into the book.

Please reach out to me if you disagree with my selection of tools and ways of working with benefits and change, if you want to share some alternatives, or if you have used the book successfully to realise more benefits. I look forward to these conversations.

If you are about to embark on the benefits realisation journey and need some advice, I would love to hear from you. This book is hardly the end of the line for our knowledge on how to best to create value in projects, and the sooner we share our experience, the faster we can take the next steps on the journey.

Whatever you do, do something! If you only read the book and do not change your behaviour, you will not benefit from your reading.

Rasmus Rytter
Copenhagen, April 2022

Part I

Introduction

1

Introduction to the Book

Benefits realisation is a method for creating the greatest possible value from a change project. It is a new way of looking at and working with business change projects and other efforts needed to develop an organisation.

> *The current focus within both public and private sectors on implementing enablers, rather than on realising benefits and achieving the vision or end goal, is so widespread and deep rooted that it needs a clear process and sustained effort to change.*
>
> Gerald Bradley, author of *Benefit Realisation Management* (2010)

Benefits realisation is about focusing on the purpose and benefits we want to achieve and the behavioural change it will require of our colleagues. The method enables us to initiate our projects by designing business change projects (which will from this point on be referred to as 'projects') to create the prerequisites for realising our desired purpose and benefits.

New Behaviour Creates Benefits

The benefits realisation method prioritises behavioural change as the decisive and triggering factor for creating value. The method shows how our colleagues' new way of working creates the desired value. This ability to couple benefits and new behaviours is key to the success of a project. Changing our colleagues' behaviour often requires help. This help is what projects are all about. It could be helping colleagues to continue working in a new way or to overcome their resistance to change. But it could also be helping to support our colleagues in attaining new competencies or create new technical deliverables in the form of processes, IT systems, or products available. The processes, the IT system, and the products are essential but are only part of the means – not the goal. The goal is benefits realisation. In addition to the technical deliverables, we must also build competencies and anchor the new behaviour before reaching our goal.

Among companies and public organisations, there is an ever-growing awareness that value creation is about more than just producing deliverables. Words such as 'value', 'effect', and 'benefits' have found their way into our language when we talk about topics such as projects, creating a greater focus on what value we need to create for our organisation, our customers, or the citizens we want to help. And yet, the practical approach to projects is still characterised by Gerald Bradley's quote above: we focus far too much on deliverables and far too little on change and benefits. There is a growing awareness among project practitioners of the importance of benefits realisation, and a common language for it is steadily developing. However, most organisations still need to define what a focus on value means and integrate a practical approach to benefits realisation and change as part of the way we develop our organisations.[1] That is what this book aims to do.

The Structure of the Book

The book consists of five parts. Each part details how to get more out of your projects. You are already well on your way with Part 1, which gives you an overview of key concepts, roles, and introduces the benefit-driven change model that visualises what it takes to create value during a project's lifetime.

The first purpose of the book is to provide a practical and case-based guide on how your organisation can get more value out of your projects. This is detailed in Part 2 and Part 3 of the book. To make it easy for you to apply the content of the book to your project or organisation's project model, the structure of the book reflects the main phases of most projects: an analysis phase (Part 2 of the book) and an execution phase (Part 3 of the book). The book's points are elaborated on through two cases from Nykredit (a large Danish financial company) and the University of Copenhagen, respectively, and detailed descriptions of the most important workshops and activities. Whether your organisation's approach to producing technical deliverables is agile, waterfall, PRINCE2, scrum, or SAFe (scaled agile framework), the way we work with benefits realisation and change management does not change significantly. Nevertheless, as it turns out, the combination with SAFe requires a little extra attention. I will go into this in Part 3.

[1] University of Oxford, Saïd Business School, and Implement Consulting Group (2015–2020). This study shows that most organisations today formulate targets for the desired outcomes of their projects. However, only one in four organisations puts figures on what the project should achieve, and less than one-fifth follow up on whether the benefit targets are achieved.

While Parts 2 and 3 illustrate what it takes to realise more benefits at the project level, Part 4 of the book shows how the benefit-driven portfolio management office (PMO) function can ensure benefits realisation across the portfolio. As soon as we broaden the use of a practical and structured approach to benefits realisation and behavioural change, we get new data on both benefits and the change effort. This enables us to manage and prioritise our portfolio in order to make decisions at the portfolio level that will maximise our benefits realisation.

Part 5 details the book's second purpose: making the benefits realisation method a part of your way of working with projects. There is more than one way of doing that, but the most successful approaches to implementing the benefits realisation method are similar in several ways. One of the organisations that have been successful in implementing the benefits realisation method is Ørsted. Ørsted is a large international renewable energy company, and the company is used as a case study on how to implement the benefits realisation method successfully. But first, you will get a brief introduction to what benefits are and a presentation of the benefit-driven change model, which sets the overall framework for benefits realisation and behavioural change. Additionally, I will introduce a number of the concepts I use along the way in the book.

The Benefit-driven Change Model

The benefits realisation method is an addition to our current technically focused (business change) projects. An additional layer that contains a practical approach to benefits realisation and behavioural change, building on an often well-established and good practice of producing technical deliverables.

In most projects, technical deliverables are just as important as changing behaviour and realising benefits to create the desired value. I will leave it to others to describe the most efficient way of producing technical deliverables and instead focus on how technical deliverables contribute to creating value.

We will use the benefit-driven change model shown in Figure 1.1 to illustrate the tasks a project should include to realise the potential benefits. The benefit-driven change model shows the project from the time its analysis phase is kicked off to after it has been completed. In the analysis phase, we design the project to create value, and the most important step in creating the benefit-driven project design is a benefits realisation workshop. Here we outline the desired benefits and what it takes to realise them. The model shows the three tracks that illustrate the main tasks of the projects, namely the benefit track, the change track, and the technical track.

The Interaction Between the Tracks

The benefit-driven project design is the starting point for the analysis phase (Part 2 of the book), where the content of the three tracks is detailed. Based on that, we will be able to create a business case and decide whether the project should proceed or not. If the project proceeds, the execution phase will require work to be done in all three project tracks as well (Part 3 of the book). Changes in the project's environment and new knowledge make it necessary to continually adjust and optimise all three tracks to maximise the project's benefits realisation. Once the last technical deliverable is produced and the desired behavioural change in the organisation is attained, the project is completed.

The only task in the realisation phase is to follow up on the realisation of the project's benefits. The follow-up on benefits realisation continues until we are confident that value creation is firmly anchored in the business (follow-up on benefits realisation takes place at the portfolio level and is described in Part 4 of the book). In projects with more than one launch, that is more

Figure 1.1 The benefit-driven change model.

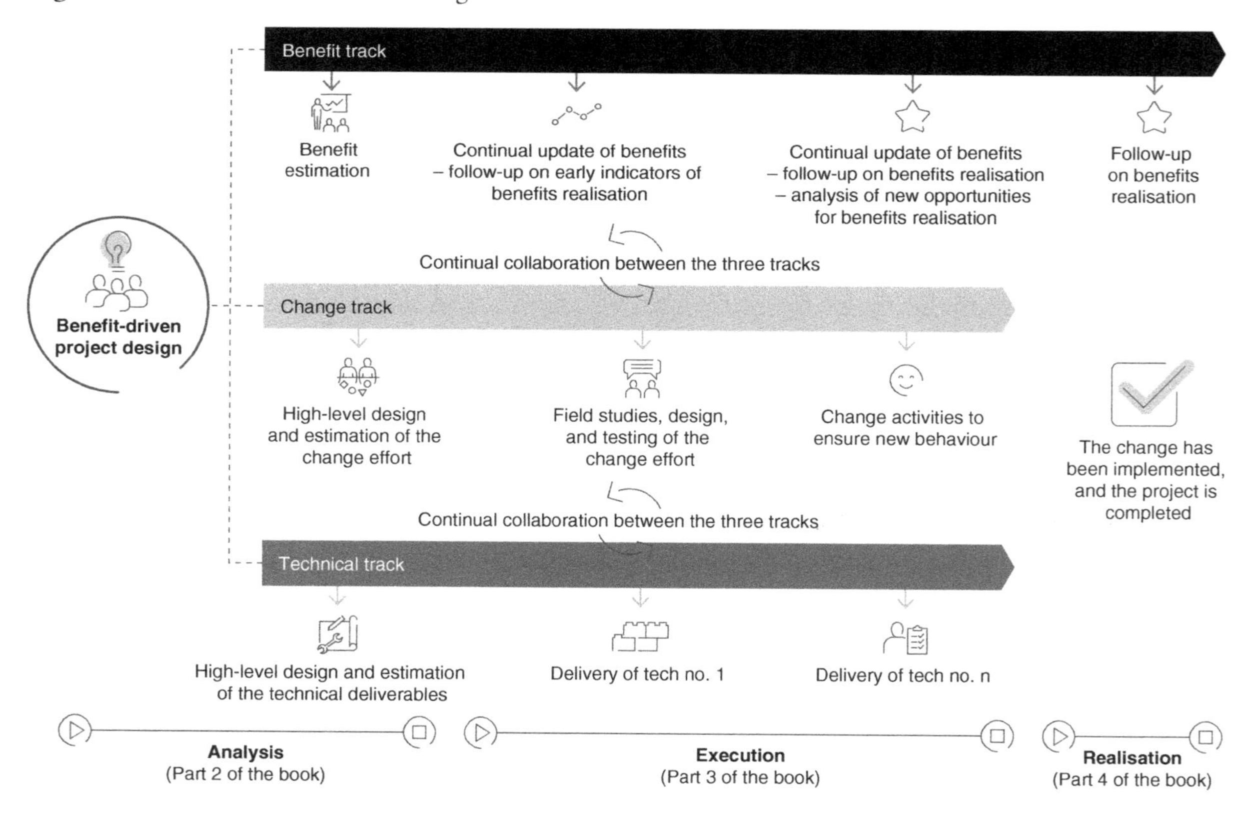

than one effort to anchor a new way of working in the organisation, the follow-up on benefits realisation starts after the first launch when the project is still in the execution phase.

The Definition of a Benefit

At this point, I have already mentioned the word 'benefit' many times. So, before we go any further, it is important to define what a benefit is.

> **Definition of a Benefit**
>
> A benefit is the result of a change that is considered positive by one or more stakeholders.

These benefits may, for example, include increased revenue or savings in either time or money. Or they may consist of increased job satisfaction, more subject matter expertise, or a better image. They are typically quantifiable, although the task of quantifying them can be so extensive that it is not feasible in practice. Benefits can be both intentional and unintentional. If one or more stakeholders considers the result of a change as negative, it is a negative benefit.

> **Definition of a Negative Benefit**
>
> A negative benefit is the result of a change that is considered negative by one or more stakeholders.

Indirect Benefits

The benefits that are most often included in a business case are those directly derived from the change implemented by the project. In many cases, projects also create indirect benefits. These are benefits that strengthen the organisation's ability to change, i.e. to create change and realise benefits in the future, although these benefits are often not quantifiable. When an organisation decides to carry out a major project without having the capabilities to succeed, building that capability for change can be unbelievably valuable. In some cases, it may even have greater value than the direct, measurable benefits of the project.

The indirect benefits are typically greatest in large-scale projects or, for example, projects where we also change the organisation's ability to carry out future projects using new methods. Here we should identify and include the indirect benefits in our business case, even though we may not be able to quantify them. In most other projects, the indirect benefits are of minor importance.

The Roles in Benefits Realisation

Before we delve into the practice of realising benefits, it is important to understand the consequences of introducing the benefits realisation method to the various roles in projects.

The book takes an offset in the project organisation and the roles many organisations are already using.

The introduction of the benefits realisation method gives project managers and leaders in the steering committee significantly more responsibility. A practical approach to benefits realisation and change as an additional layer to our projects also impacts the PMO function that facilitates portfolio management.

Many organisations that have already implemented a structured approach to benefits realisation and change have method specialists supporting project managers and steering committee members in performing the new tasks related to realising benefits and change efforts. The method specialist role can be inside or outside the PMO. When the benefits realisation method is fully implemented, there is typically a close coupling of the finance department and the PMO, creating a direct link between realised benefits and the organisation's budgets if the benefits are of a financial nature.

The traditional project organisation has proven to be highly effective at ensuring the production of technical deliverables. Thus, the goal is to expand the roles and responsibilities in the project organisation to make it just as skilled in ensuring organisational change and benefits realisation as when ensuring the production of technical deliverables. The key roles in the project organisation are illustrated in Figure 1.2.

The Role of the PMO Function

A project is either formally or informally part of a portfolio. The role of the PMO is to ensure that the portfolio's benefit potential

Figure 1.2 Key roles in the project organisation.

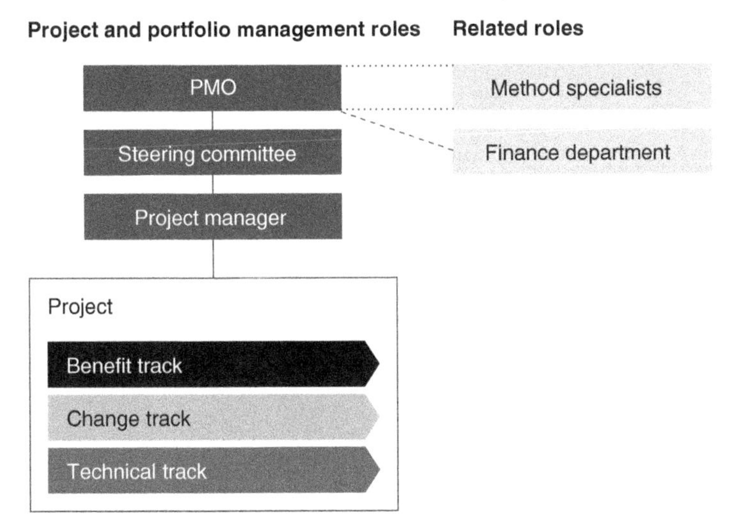

is realised. To succeed in this, the PMO undertakes several tasks. First, the PMO must facilitate management's prioritisation of the portfolio. It includes establishing a basis for decision-making for prioritisation, which should be based on project data. To do so effectively, it is necessary to govern how decisions are made at the project and portfolio level and balance the capacity available to develop projects. In cases where the PMO is also responsible for providing support to the projects, the responsibility may include providing training and practical assistance to the projects so that project managers and managers can receive coaching, facilitation support, or other project-related services.

The Steering Committee and the Role of the Benefit Owner

The definition of a benefit as 'a result of a change that is considered positive by one or more stakeholders' indicates an owner of the benefits. A person who is prepared to take ownership for realising a benefit on behalf of themselves or a group of stakeholders. That person is called a benefit owner.

The benefit-driven steering committee has two roles, as illustrated in Figure 1.3: the benefit owner role and the supplier role. There can be more than one benefit owner in the steering

Figure 1.3 The benefit-driven steering committee.

Project owner
Primary benefit owner

Secondary benefit
owner(s) (if needed)

Supplier

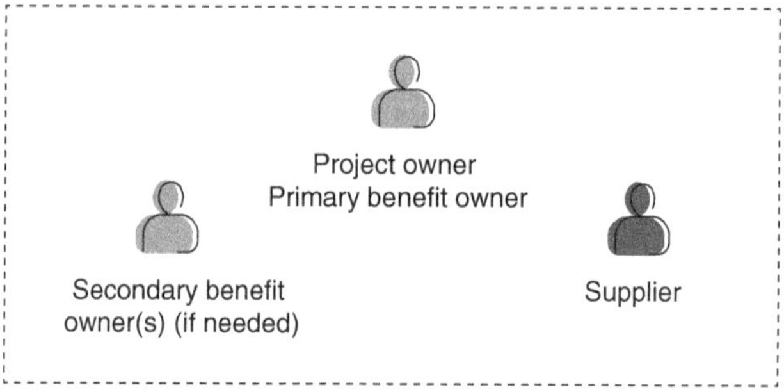

committee, and the leader of the steering committee is called a project owner. The project owner is the primary benefit owner, i.e. the benefit owner who has the most at stake. This person is also responsible for the overall business case in addition to the responsibility for benefits realisation.

The benefit owner role is new and, at the same time, essential. The benefit owner is a person or representative of the people owning the project benefits. Thus, the benefit owner defines the desired benefits, follows up on whether they can still be realised, looks for new opportunities for realising benefits, and reports on the benefits to the PMO after the project is completed.

> In the benefit-driven steering committee, all benefits must be owned by one of the steering committee members. If we allow benefits without owners, the risk that the benefits will never be realised is far too great.

The benefit owner has the overall responsibility for ensuring that the change driving the benefits realisation process will occur. The benefit owner also acts as a promoter of the change and is thus highly active in the project.

In projects or programmes where benefits are realised across organisations, sharing the benefit ownership with sub-benefit owners makes good sense. It anchors the change efforts and benefits locally and eases the workload of the steering committee. The number of participants in the steering committee can thus be kept at a level that makes it possible to get together and make decisions at short notice. Figure 1.4 outlines the delegation of benefit ownership.

Additionally, the benefit owner usually supplies resources to the benefit track and change track coming from their part of the organisation.

Figure 1.4 Delegation of benefit ownership.

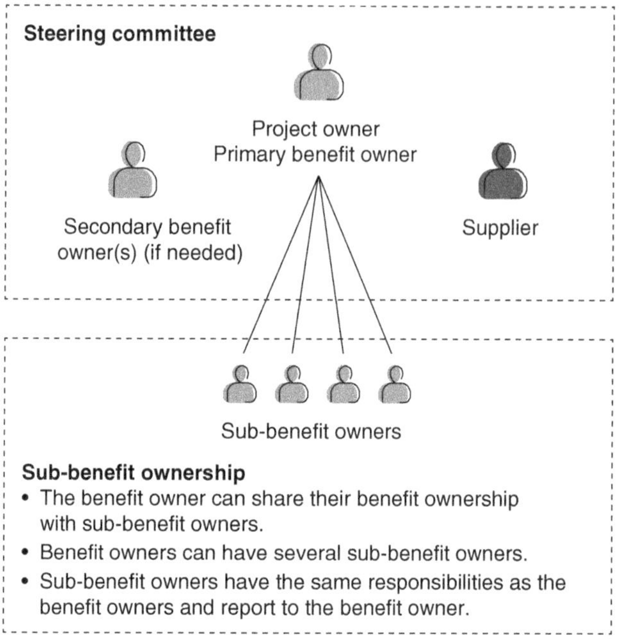

Steering committee

Project owner
Primary benefit owner

Secondary benefit owner(s) (if needed)

Supplier

Sub-benefit owners

Sub-benefit ownership

- The benefit owner can share their benefit ownership with sub-benefit owners.
- Benefit owners can have several sub-benefit owners.
- Sub-benefit owners have the same responsibilities as the benefit owners and report to the benefit owner.

Large-scale projects often require IT or technical deliverables from internal or external suppliers. It is important to maintain the traditional supplier role for the steering committee to ensure the efficient production of technical deliverables. The responsibility of a supplier in the steering committee is to make sure that the technical deliverables meet the agreed requirements for time, quality, and cost.[2]

The Project Manager Role

Project managers face changes that alter what a project contains and the criteria for doing well in the project manager role.

[2]The traditional supplier role is described in PRINCE2 (Office of Government Commerce 2009).

The steering committee no longer has only the management responsibility for a project producing technical deliverables. Likewise, the project manager is not responsible only for managing a team producing technical deliverables. The project manager is responsible for a team that always has an updated picture of what benefits it can realise. The project manager also analyses and executes the organisational change and produces the technical deliverables needed for the benefit owner to realise the benefits.

In order to be successful with benefits realisation in a project, the benefit owners and the project manager must fulfil their new roles. While the role of the benefit owner is primarily about taking greater responsibility for the benefits and change efforts and thus being more involved in the project, it is different for the project manager. The project manager's new role includes a significant expansion of the responsibilities and subject matter area that projects now include. Benefits realisation and organisational change are crafts: it takes time to get good at them.

Some project managers will take their project management skills to a new level and become specialists in working with benefits realisation and change efforts. Others will become project managers of larger projects containing a series of subprojects with more specialised project managers or project participants responsible for technology development or organisational change. In contrast, others will specialise as, for example, IT project managers or change managers. Regardless of which path the organisation and the individual project manager choose to take, it is crucial for the project's benefits realisation that the new tasks in the project manager role are performed.

Method Specialists

Visualising the project's three tracks from the benefit-driven change model creates a need to implement benefits realisation

Table 1.1 Roles, responsibilities and tasks in the benefit realisation process.

Role	Benefit realisation responsibility	Benefit realisation task	Who in the organisation
Top management	Responsible for realising the strategy, including maximising the benefit realisation through the projects in the portfolio.	Makes the decisions that realise the organisation's strategy and maximise benefit realisation.	Company management. Either the top management or possibly the management of a business unit.
PMO/ portfolio office	Responsible for facilitating and implementing the top management's prioritisation of the portfolio.	Prepares the basis for decision-making and ensures the start-up of the projects that give the organisation the greatest possible benefits measured against the objectives laid down in the strategy. Ensures that different projects are not chasing the same benefits and collects data for benefit realisation and change at the portfolio level.	PMO/portfolio unit.
Project owner/ primary benefit owner (steering committee role)	Accountable for the entire project and business case, including benefit realisation.	Ensures benefit realisation and organisational change for the entire project, including that any shared benefit realisation responsibility is firmly rooted in sub-benefit owners who are not part of the steering committee.	Top or senior manager in the part of the business where (most of) the benefits are realised.
Benefit owner (steering committee role)	Accountable for realising benefits and for the organisational change that benefit realisation requires. Supplier of resources for the change effort.	Ensures benefit realisation and is a promoter of the organisational change in his or her part of the business. In addition, the benefit owner must validate that the benefits remain achievable during the project and monitor opportunities for new benefits. Reports on benefit realisation during the project and after the project is completed.	Manager in the part of the business where (most of) the benefits are realised.

Supplier (steering committee role)	Accountable for the technical deliverables meeting the requirements of the business so that the business can realise benefits.	Ensures that technical deliverables are delivered at the agreed time, quality and cost.	Head of IT department, external supplier.
Project manager	Responsible for managing the project so that it creates the possibility of benefit realisation.	Day-to-day management of the project, including management of the benefit track, change track and technical track. Supports the benefit owner by continuously helping to identify opportunities that could increase benefit realisation and risks that could reduce it.	Typical part of the business or a central project management organisation.
Finance department	Responsible for transferring realised and planned benefits into the organisation's budgets.	Ongoing dialogue with the PMO function about future budgeting based on the expected future benefit realisation and actual adjustment of budgets based on realised benefits.	The finance department.
Method specialists	Ownership of and responsible for continuous development of the benefit realisation and change methods, including training in and support for the use of the methods.	Ensures continuous updating of methods, competency development and ad hoc support for project managers and steering committee members.	Experienced project manager who also works as a method specialist or a PMO employee with project experience.

and change management in the way we work with projects. This gives rise to expanding the project method framework, so the new benefit and change methods get an owner and are continually updated.

Anchoring benefits realisation and behavioural change among method specialists, who master the new methods and can pass it on in the organisation, has proven to be an effective way to implement benefits realisation and behavioural change. *After* an implementation, many organisations choose to retain the method specialists, partly to ensure the future development of the methods and partly to continually improve the competencies of new and current project managers. Thus, the method specialists provide a permanent service offering training, coaching, and practical facilitation assistance to project managers and benefit owners. Being a method specialist is often a small part of their job alongside their primary role as, for example, a project manager.

In Table 1.1, you will find a complete overview of the roles in and around the project.

You now have the foundation to get started with what this book is all about: to provide you with a practical and case-based guide to creating more value through your projects. We begin where the project has just been kicked off.

Part II

Designing the Change

2

A New Way of Initiating Projects

If we start by agreeing on the value we aim to create, we have taken a big step in the right direction.

Start with the end in mind.

Steve Jenner, author of
Managing Benefits (2014)

If we start by agreeing on the title of a new deliverable, we are postponing many important conversations. We may get going a lot faster and satisfy the need to say, 'We are up and running' to the person in senior management who owns the project. The problem is that the conversations we postpone do not just go away. They re-emerge, and the dialogue about why we are proceeding with the project and what benefits should come out of it will not be shorter or less complicated by being postponed – on the contrary.

We need to start by setting the right direction for the project and clarifying the desired change. In that way, we give the project the best possible foundation for successful implementation. Furthermore, we save the project, the steering committee, and its surroundings many detours and frustrations later in the process. It requires that we invest in conducting workshops and using the working hours required. It also requires that we get the benefit and cost estimates, making it possible to make an informed choice about initiating the project and setting the right direction (Figure 2.1).

The Analysis Phase

Before the analysis phase, the first step includes screening and evaluating ideas, keeping only the most promising ones. This chapter assumes that we have already completed this process. In the analysis phase, we then create the foundation for deciding whether to proceed with the project.

To illustrate the activities in the analysis phase, we will use the benefit-driven change model that I introduced in Chapter 1 (Figure 1.1). The model shows the project lifecycle from the time an idea turns into a project, i.e. from the beginning of the analysis phase. The analysis phase on the far left of the model in Figure 2.2 first includes designing the project to realise benefits. After this, the remaining tasks in the analysis phase can be divided into three tracks with different, but equally important, types of tasks to be solved in the project. This is illustrated by the three parallel arrows in the model.

In the rest of Part 2, I will go through how the tasks in the analysis phase may be performed to create the best conditions for creating value with the project. First, I will go over the task of designing the project, which can be divided into two steps: developing the purpose and the benefits realisation workshop. Next up are the tasks in the benefit track and change track. Along the way, I will walk through the strong links to the tasks in the technical track.

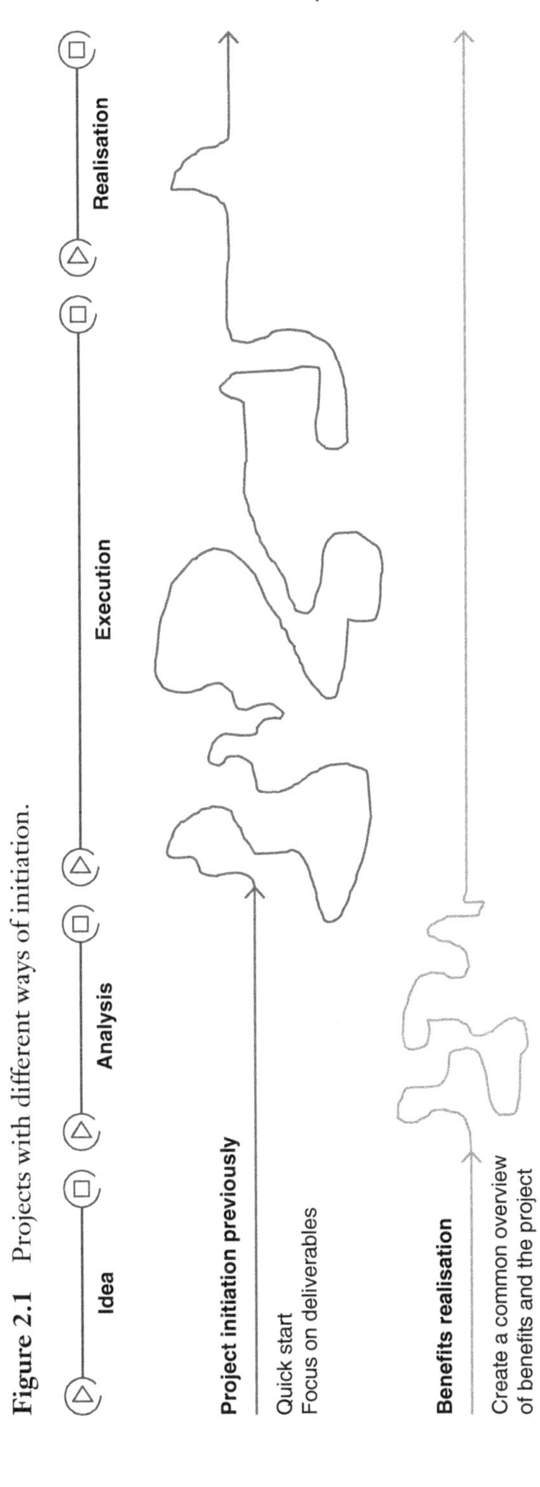

Figure 2.1 Projects with different ways of initiation.

Source: Based on Olsson et al. (2018).

Figure 2.2 Tasks in the analysis phase.

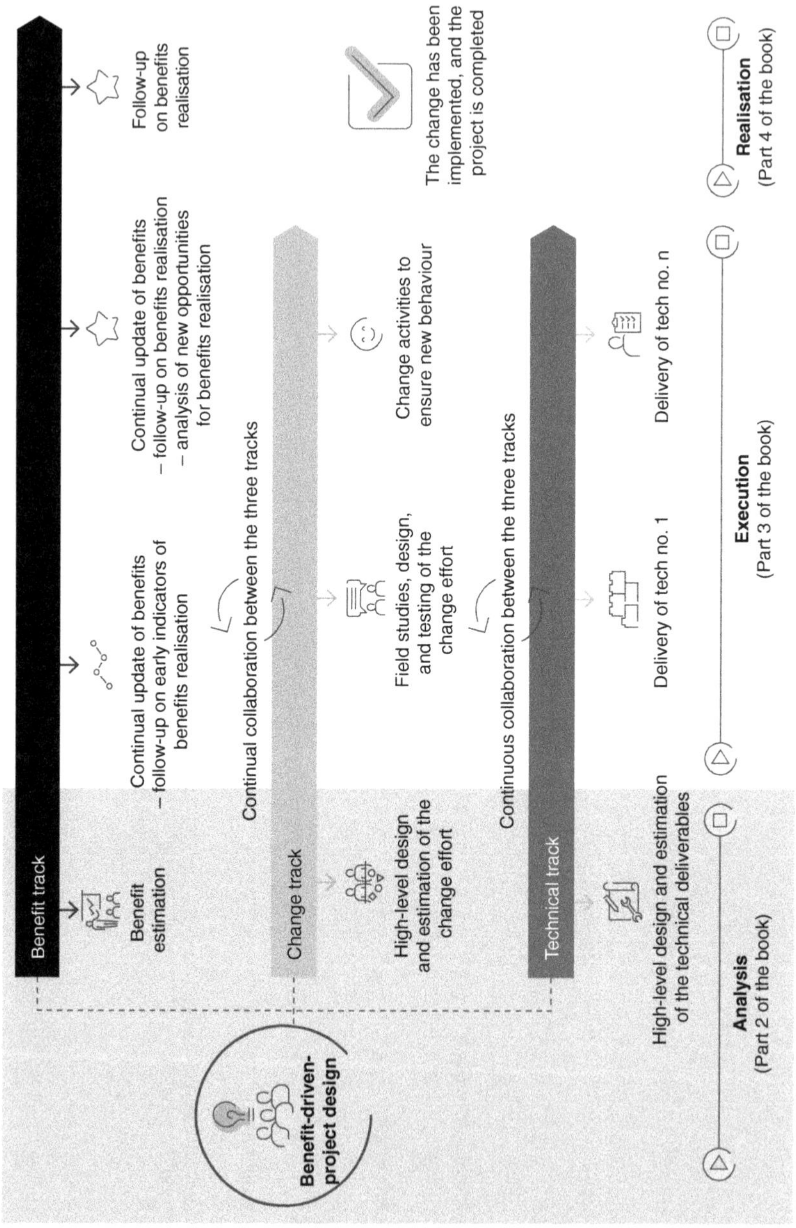

3

Developing the Purpose

You will not find many people who think the purpose of a project is insignificant. On the other hand, it is not easy to agree on what a purpose consists of for a specific project.

I often ask the question: 'What is the purpose of the project?' to project managers and benefit owners. Every other time, I get the answer: 'The purpose of the project is to produce [insert technical deliverable].' I want to make it clear right away: the purpose is *never* to develop a new IT system, process, product, or other forms of technical deliverables. Instead, the purpose of a project is to help the organisation realise part of its strategy. So, for a project to be considered part of the organisation's portfolio, it must create value that helps it realise its strategic goals.

The Project's Contribution to the Strategy

Figure 3.1 shows the connection between an organisation's strategic purposes and the purposes that each project contributes to realising. Each project can have one or more purposes, and in the figure each project contributes to realising the overall strategy,

Figure 3.1 The connection between project purposes and strategic purposes.

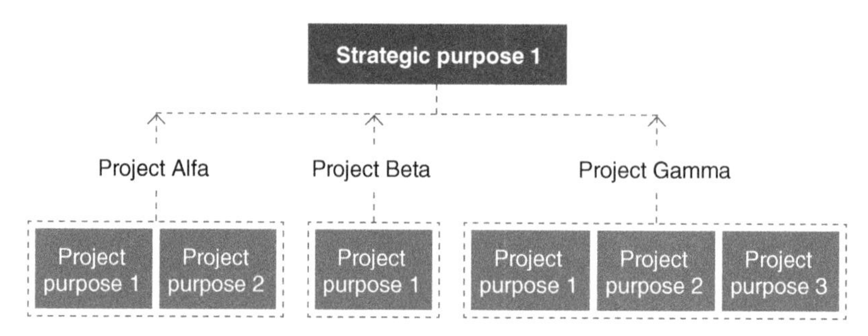

which is called 'strategic purposes'. The figure is simplified, as a project in some cases contributes to several strategic purposes, while in others there may be levels of purposes between the project level and the strategic level.

From a benefits realisation perspective, the purpose of each project can be defined by the purpose equation.

The Purpose Equation

Purpose = Value + Boundaries

Overall, the values a project is chasing can be divided into four categories (Table 3.1).

Each purpose in a project relates to one of the categories. The four categories may be interdependent. For example, greater customer satisfaction (stakeholder satisfaction) leads to an increase in revenue.

When defining a project's purposes, the value categories help clarify what type of value we are chasing in the project. Are we introducing robots into the passport office to free up time to provide citizens with a better service (stakeholder satisfaction)?

Table 3.1 Value categories of the project purpose.

Value category	Includes purposes, such as
Revenue	• Increasing revenue • Avoiding or reducing the risk of a decrease in revenue
Costs	• Reducing costs • Avoiding or reducing the risk of increased costs
Compliance	• Ensuring continued authorisation to operate • Avoiding regulatory fines
Stakeholder satisfaction	• Achieving greater stakeholder satisfaction • Avoiding or reducing the risk of dissatisfied stakeholders

Or are we looking to cut payroll costs? Or do we have to comply with new legislation on speeding up case processing time (compliance)? This clarification is essential for how we design the rest of the project and should therefore be done immediately.

The purpose also defines the scope of the project. For example, if we are to generate more revenue, what are we allowed to do? Should the extra revenue come from selling more of our current products in Denmark? Can we open a sales office in the Baltics? Or buy a competitor in Belgium? If we want to improve patient satisfaction, should we then focus on patient involvement or use private hospitals to reduce waiting lists – or are both options?

With both value and scope in place, we have what we need to formulate our purpose from a benefits realisation perspective.

Motivation to Change

From a change perspective, we should preferably add something. If we can engage colleagues who will spend a large part of their workday on the project, and perhaps also those who are going to change their ways of working because of the project, then we must do so. If we can add an element that gives our colleagues the feeling that the purpose makes sense, we are already well on the way to ensuring buy-in to support the change. In other words, we need to chase a purpose that does not just focus on value and the scope of the project. We must try to formulate a purpose that will be a lever for the change.

The motivational purpose equation that helps us create change and benefits realisation is defined like this:

The Motivational Purpose Equation

Motivational purpose = Value + Boundaries
+ Positive emotional response

The positive emotional response rarely comes from arguments about finance and compliance alone. To create the best possible positive emotional response among those working on projects, we must communicate the value we create for the project's stakeholders. If the purpose of the project is to create value for a group of stakeholders, we may already have succeeded. If not, we can either find input for the purpose that gives the positive emotional response among the project's stakeholders or move up a level and find input in the strategic purposes the project supports.

The important thing about a motivational purpose is that it is credible. Suppose we create an efficiency project that causes one in four customer service employees to lose their jobs. In that case, we must be careful not to create a purpose that becomes untrustworthy in pursuit of a motivational purpose. After all, it is not for the sake of the customer service employees we carry out the project. If we are not honest about why we are carrying out the project, it becomes untrustworthy and has the opposite effect: it becomes demotivating. If it is to ensure the company's long-term survival, it can be included in the purpose. If we want to upgrade the competencies of our customer service employees to stay ahead in a digital future, it is even better.

The rule of thumb is that, when we are primarily chasing a revenue or cost purpose, it is important to consider whether it is necessary to sacrifice part of the project's financial benefits to achieve a purpose that creates value for all the project's stakeholders. This sharing of the benefits between the organisation and its employees, customers, or users may be necessary to bring about the change needed for the organisation to realise its benefits.

The Practical Development of the Purpose

Since the purpose sets the direction and boundaries for the project and can ease the efforts associated with the organisational change, it is worth spending time developing it in the right way.

If the purpose lies in continuation of the strategy the organisation is working to achieve, you are already well underway. In other situations, less is given in advance. When there is a need to define value, boundaries, and the positive emotional response, it is often easiest to start with value and boundaries. Once the logical, rational part is in place, and it is clear what value we want to create for which stakeholders, we can begin to add the positive emotional part.

Five Important Questions

The purpose can be developed using a series of facilitation questions for each of the three parameters on the right side of the motivational purpose equation. The conversation around the purpose should evolve around five important questions covering all parameters of the equation's right-hand side.

To uncover the value, ask the following questions:

1. What problem or opportunity should the project solve or achieve?
2. What benefits can we achieve by solving the problem or seizing the opportunity (see value categories in Table 3.1)?

Problems and opportunities can be two sides of the same coin. If the processing time of an application for unemployment benefit is long, it can be a problem if caseworkers cannot process the cases within the agreed time. It may also be an opportunity to free up time for other tasks that are not currently being solved. Similarly, the statement 'The fact that there are currently no products on the Swedish market that create the same value as our new product range' may be an opportunity to increase revenue. However, launching the new product line in Sweden may also be a way to avoid leaving a market opportunity that a competitor could use to gain a foothold in the Scandinavian market. Once we agree on the problem we want to solve or what opportunity we want to seize, it is easier to identify which value categories the project's benefits are in.

Boundaries are uncovered by discussing:

1. What are the expected boundaries of the project (e.g. geographical, organisational, employee groups, segments)?

The above question ensures that we discuss the conditions of the project and thus get the guidance we need about how creative we can be when pursuing the benefits we discussed in Question 2. All the various examples of boundaries may, in principle, be relevant to discuss. However, in practice, not everything may be relevant. Therefore, let the examples above act as inspiration and only select the boundaries that are relevant to discuss in your specific project. When we talk about boundaries, it is a balance between defining what the project cannot deviate from without eliminating any opportunities that may help the project to create more value.

When defining the boundaries, the rule of thumb is to avoid going into too much detail and only eliminate options that we know for sure will be irrelevant.

Creating a positive emotional response is the first take on the heart of the story that will help us create a demand for the project and what the project delivers. You should ask the following questions:

1. What value do we create for the three groups of employees who are affected the most?
2. What value do we create for external stakeholders?

If the primary value of the project relates to stakeholder satisfaction, the last questions may already have been answered. If the primary purpose of the project is to create economic value or ensure compliance, it is important to establish what value the project creates for the employees and managers affected by it.

At this stage, if it is difficult to identify any value for the colleagues going through the change, it should be discussed if the idea for the project is good and if it is possible to implement. At the very least, it should be an attention point in relation to the further work with the project and the challenges this might create in getting their colleagues to change their ways of working. The five questions along with a space for the phrasing the purpose is illustrated in a poster format in Figure 3.2.

Phrasing the Purpose

When the five questions have been answered, the next step is to phrase the purpose. If the primary purpose of the project is to create economic value or ensure compliance, it is equally as important to make it clear what value it will create for the

Figure 3.2 Developing the purpose.

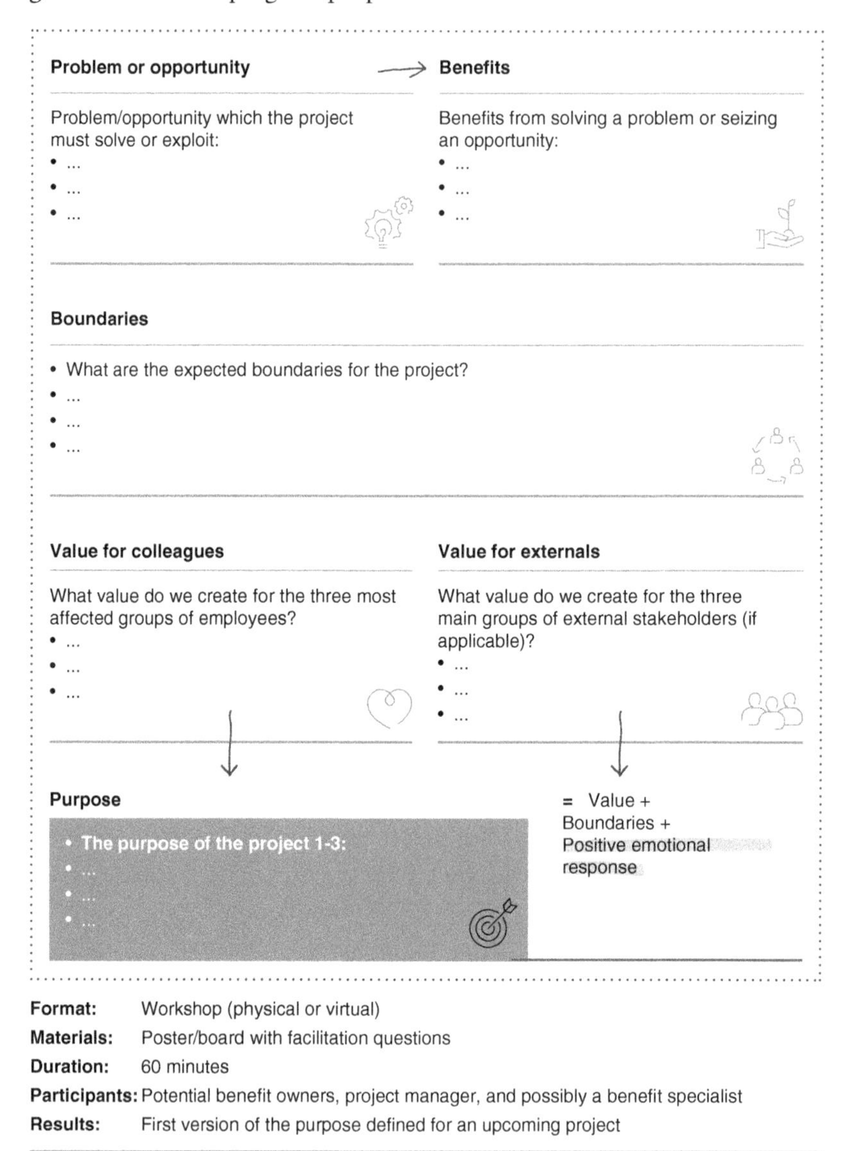

Format: Workshop (physical or virtual)
Materials: Poster/board with facilitation questions
Duration: 60 minutes
Participants: Potential benefit owners, project manager, and possibly a benefit specialist
Results: First version of the purpose defined for an upcoming project

Source: Inspired by Helle Falholt.

employees and managers who will be impacted. If the project has more than three purposes, it should be considered if it is perhaps a programme with several related projects.

Purposes are not measurable. Examples of purposes include creating revenue growth, reducing costs, complying with legislation, or increasing employee satisfaction. We talk about the types of value we want to create, without putting any actual numbers on them, as this is part of defining the benefits.

The task of phrasing a purpose can easily get a little out of hand and take a very long time if we do not go about it in a structured manner. Therefore, review the motivational purpose equation, put the five facilitation questions up on a board or poster like in Figure 3.2, and go through them one by one. When phrasing the purpose, aim for an 80% solution as a starting point for the benefits realisation workshop described in Chapter 4. You will often receive new inputs for the purpose along the way, so put off making the final 'perfect' formulation until it is communicated outside the project.

For the rest of this chapter and in Chapters 4 and 5, I will use a case (Nykredit Business Bank) to exemplify how we work with the purpose, and discuss how to design the project including a step-by-step guide to unfolding the benefits. This ensures that we finish the analysis phase with credible benefit estimates and a clear picture of how they will be realised.

Case: Nykredit Business Bank

Nykredit started working with benefits realisation and the benefits realisation method back in 2015. They wanted to use the benefits realisation method for a new corporate banking concept, Nykredit Business Bank. Nykredit Business Bank was aimed at small and medium-sized owner-managed businesses. Nykredit wanted to offer a value proposition that focused on the owner instead of the business. Thus, Nykredit offered to handle both business and personal finances for this group of business owners.

Nykredit had identified a segment of people with smaller owner-managed businesses whose needs were not met and who altogether did not receive much attention from either their competitors or Nykredit. Their business and personal finances were often closely integrated. Still, they were met by two different parts of the bank, depending on whether business or private finances was at the top of the agenda. By offering these business owners a value proposition that included both business and personal finances, the bank could increase its revenue and earnings and provide the customers with better services and prices.

Organisationally, it would mean a large change. New teams of financial advisers would be formed, primarily consisting of advisers who had previously served personal banking or business customers. They were to switch jobs in Nykredit and be trained to help the owner-managed segment, and this was to be done without disrupting the rest of the organisation's operations.

At this early stage, there was uncertainty as to how the advisers would receive the new job profile. How many would want this new job? They would be spending a much larger part of their workday on sales than on servicing customers. Thus, the purpose focused on capturing a new segment (owner-managers in small and medium-sized businesses) to create a more positive response among the advisers. In addition, it was expected that owner-managers would welcome the new value proposition, as this would make managing their finances easier and give them better prices.

Nykredit's choice of a strategic purpose as an umbrella for the projects that were to bring Nykredit Business Bank to life was ultimately formulated broadly by its management team as: 'Nykredit is to be the preferred financial partner of owner-managers.'

The projects that were to realise the strategic purpose had the following purposes:

- We want to capture the owner-manager segment (revenue purpose).
- We want to create the greatest value for the customer (stakeholder satisfaction purpose).

Figure 3.3 Developing a purpose: Nykredit Business Bank.

Problem or opportunity → **Benefits**

Problem/opportunity which the project must solve or exploit:

- Owner-managers have an unmet need in terms of getting advice on both business and personal finances in one place.
- Owner-managers are not a focus area at Nykredit or with Nykredit's competitors at the moment.
- It is economically attractive to have owner-managers as both business and personal banking customers in Nykredit.

Benefits from solving a problem or seizing an opportunity:

- Increased revenue and earnings.
- More satisfied and loyal owner-manager customers.

Boundaries

What are the expected boundaries for the project?

- As a general rule, the recruitment of advisers must be done from other parts of the bank.
- The project is limited to the owner-manager segment.

Value for colleagues

What value do we create for the three most affected groups of employees?

- The business bank will allow employees to work with a new growth area (expected positive response).
- It is expected to be an attractive development opportunity, especially for advisers in personal banking (expected positive response).

Value for externals

What value do we create for the three main groups of external stakeholders (if applicable)?

- Easier and better banking experience by having one adviser for all banking services.

Purpose

The purpose of the project 1-3:

- We will win the owner-manager segment (revenue purpose).
- We want to create the greatest value for the customer (stakeholder satisfaction purpose).

= Value + Boundaries + Positive emotional response

The revenue purpose did not include the word 'revenue', but no one in the organisation had any doubts as to what it was about. The boundaries consisted of the revenue coming from owner-managers as well as their businesses and the advisers having to be recruited internally.

Figure 3.3 outlines developing a purpose with regards to Nykredit Business Bank.

4

Design the Project to Realise Benefits

There are many important moments in the life of a project. For most projects, the most important one is when the project is designed, and everyone can see the benefits it will create.

At Nykredit, all projects are kicked off with a benefits realisation workshop.
Carsten Kruse, Vice President, Nykredit

Many associate project design with technology or IT architecture, but that is not the idea here. By designing the project correctly, we create a shared picture of how it will add value and what it entails.

One of the main reasons many projects fail to realise the intended value is that they are designed and executed following this process:

1. Someone in the organisation gets an idea that is converted into the purpose of a project.

2. Next, you begin designing the IT system, new product, service, process, or other technical deliverables deemed necessary for the project.
3. The project's deliverables are produced.

When the project manager has finished producing the deliverables, the project is closed, and they get a pat on the back and move on to the next project. This way of designing and executing projects is illustrated in Figure 4.1.

The approach leaves a black box between the project's deliverables and the project's purpose. If we design projects by jumping from the purpose directly into specifying and producing deliverables, we can easily get the project's deliverables produced. If the project realises benefits, we cannot manage or follow up on the benefits, as we have not defined them in detail. Even worse, we have not defined a clear image of what is required of the organisation to realise these benefits, and the effort to create the necessary change in behaviour to realise the benefits risks being left undone.

Carsten Kruse from Nykredit insists that all projects should be designed 'the right way' at a benefits realisation workshop. By now, he knows that, no matter how good the IT deliverables are, it will all be in vain if the financial advisers do not use them as intended, or even not at all. The IT system may be made of gold, but no benefits will come out of it if nobody uses it.

Figure 4.1 The black box of the benefits realisation process.

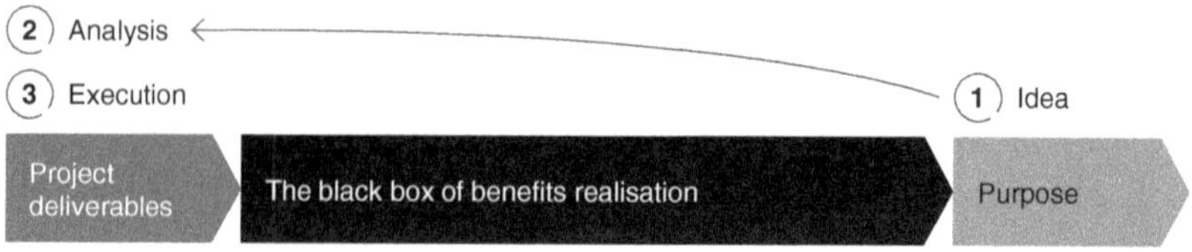

Source: Rytter et al. (2015).

The Great Focus on Deliverables

Those of us who have worked with project management for a long time have been trained to believe that a successful project equals deliverables. Since the 1960s, we have practised producing deliverables at the agreed time, cost, and quality. We know this definition of a project like the back of our hand. The keen focus on delivery has also solved both the engineer's and IT project manager's need to produce infrastructure, IT systems, and other technical deliverables. When we look at change projects that create value by changing the *way* we work, the deliverables are still important, but in themselves not nearly enough.

In addition to defining the project's deliverables, most organisations also succeed in building up competencies to use the new deliverables, for example through training. A rough guess is often made about what specific amount of money you hope to get out of the project. The challenge most people have is to detail what benefits we need to realise, what new behaviours are necessary to realise the benefits, and how to acquire the new behaviour. The fact that we more or less go directly from purpose to deliverables is the main reason our projects often fail to realise the full benefit potential. In short, there is something wrong with the way we design our projects.

The Road to Benefits Realisation

To realise the full benefit potential of our projects, we need to include all parts of the benefits realisation process when designing the project (Figure 4.2).

Figure 4.2 The benefits realisation process.

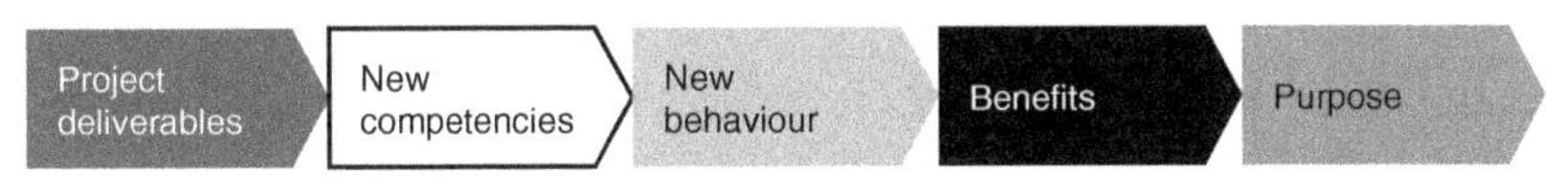

Source: Rytter et al. (2015).

The benefits realisation process visualises how projects create value and what it takes to realise the desired benefits and achieve the purpose of the project. The benefits realisation process is based on a cause-and-effect relationship. If we succeed in producing the project's deliverables and help our colleagues acquire new competencies and behavioural change, we will create the benefits needed to achieve our purpose. Thus, value creation takes place from left to right.

The Benefit Map

The benefits realisation process is the starting point for the design of the project. But while value creation takes place from left to right, the project is designed from right to left.

When designing the project, we unfold the benefits realisation process by asking six questions. The first three focus on what we want to achieve in terms of purpose, benefits, and behaviour:

1. What is the purpose of the project?
2. What benefits do we need to realise to fulfil the purpose?
3. What new behaviour do our colleagues need to attain to realise the desired benefits?

The last three questions focus on what the project must deliver:

1. What kind of support do our colleagues need in order to change their behaviour?
2. What kind of competencies are necessary for our colleagues to change their behaviour?
3. What kind of technical deliverables are required for our colleagues to change their behaviour?

The project's previous main focus – deliverables and partly acquiring new competencies – we now see as the prerequisites for what the project is really about: how do we create the change needed for the project to realise the benefits we aim to deliver? Changing behaviour has taken over as the key prerequisite for the success of the project.

Visualising the Entire Project and How to Realise the Benefits

Once we have unfolded the benefits realisation process, we get the benefit map. The benefit map is not only the key tool in our work with managing benefits. It is also the focal point for the leadership and management of the entire project. The benefit map shows the project in its entirety and visualises the cause and effect relationships in the project and thus how we expect the project to create value and achieve its purpose.

Figure 2.2 shows that the analysis phase starts with the benefit-driven project design. When designing the project, the first task is to develop the purpose, and the second and final task is the benefits realisation workshop.

The first version of the benefit map is made in the benefits realisation workshop and is based on our previous work on developing the purpose. The rest of the work in the analysis phase consists of obtaining knowledge about the individual parts of the benefit map, enabling us to estimate costs and benefits to assess whether or not to execute the project. As the benefit map is the main managerial tool within the project execution phase, it should always illustrate an updated depiction of what our project looks like, including updated expectations for the benefits we expect to realise and expectations for the project's content and costs. See the benefit map illustrated in Figure 4.3.

At the top of the benefit map are the elements of the benefits realisation process. They are identical to the benefits realisation

Figure 4.3 The benefit map.

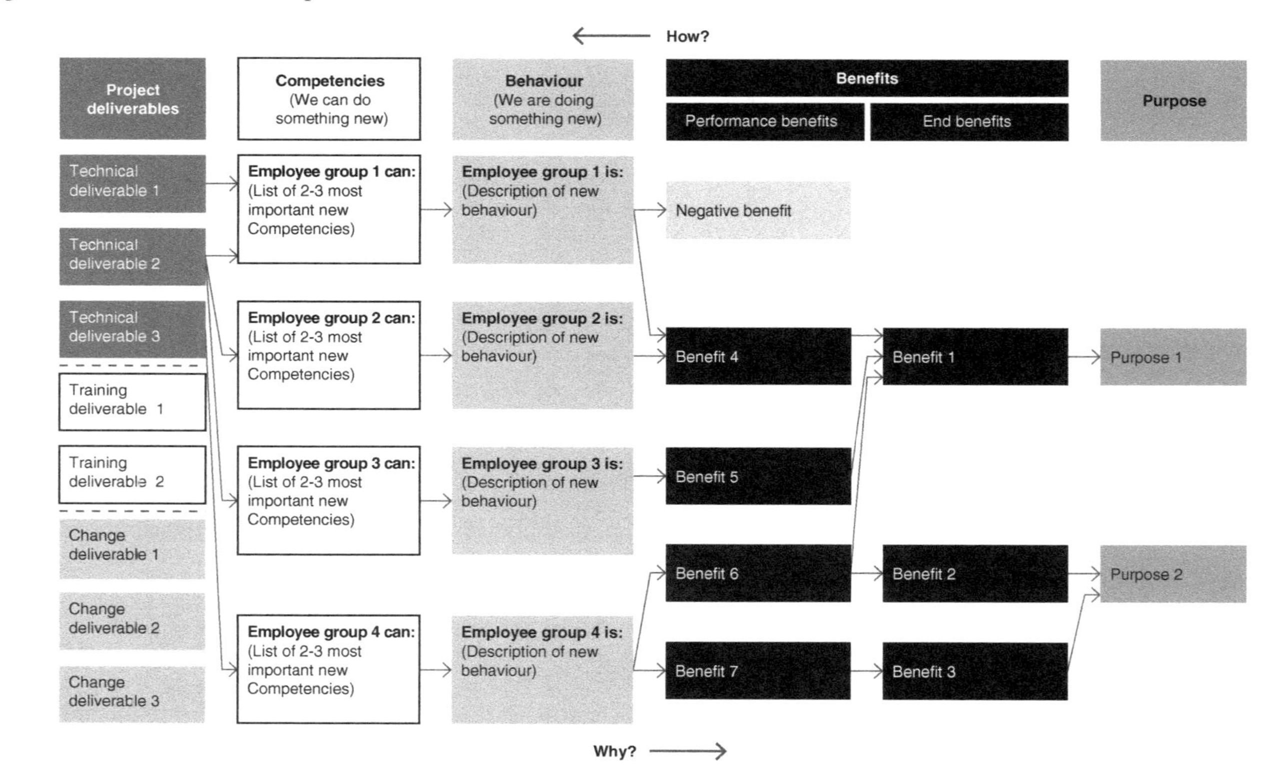

process in Figure 4.2, with the addition that benefits are divided into categories of 'end benefits' and 'performance benefits'. Benefits should be understood as positive benefits, but since projects can also generate negative benefits it is important to make them visible so we can decide how to deal with them. The main cause-and-effect relationships are shown with arrows. To explain what is required to achieve the purpose of the project, you start from the purposes defined by the project and ask 'How?' all the way to the left in the benefit map until you reach the project deliverables that contribute to achieving the purpose. If you go from left to right in the chart, you can see how each deliverable contributes to benefits and the purpose by asking 'Why?' Let us take a look at the Nykredit Business Bank case study to illustrate how you can work with the benefit map.

Case Study on Nykredit Business Bank

The first project Nykredit initiated to realise Nykredit Business Bank was a pilot project aimed at independent doctors and dentists who form a subsegment of owner-managers. The project aimed to identify whether there was a basis for launching Nykredit Business Bank to the entire owner-manager segment and at the same time realise enough benefits to constitute a good business case on its own.

The pilot project was named 'White Coats' and was designed during a benefits realisation workshop. The 'White Coats' benefit map is shown in Figure 4.4 as it looked at the end of the analysis phase after estimating benefits and validating the remaining elements of the map.

The right side of the map shows the two purposes of the project. The first purpose is to capture a new segment (revenue purpose), while the other focuses on creating the greatest value for the customer (stakeholder satisfaction purpose). In continuation of the revenue purpose, 'end benefits' have been established

Figure 4.4 The 'White Coats' benefit map (simplified).

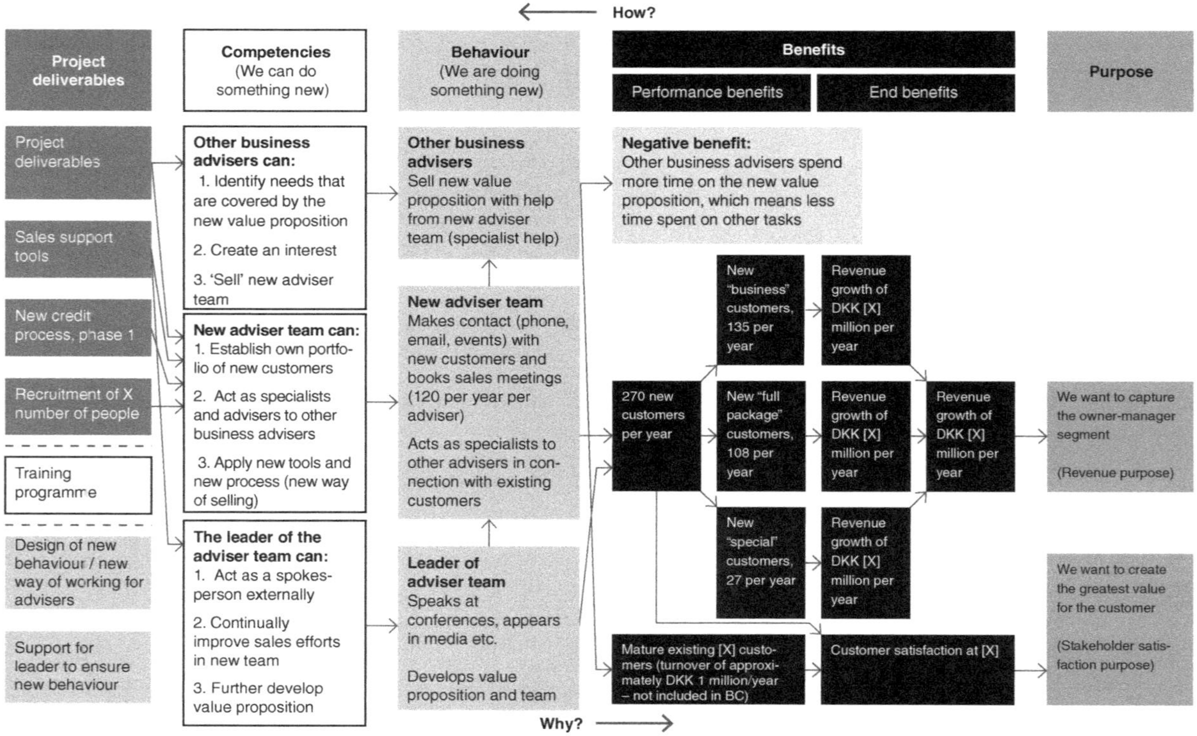

[X] covers specific figures. The number of customers is adjusted according to the correct figures.

in the form of specific revenue targets (anonymised) broken down into three subsegments. The end benefits in DKK are driven by performance benefits – in this case, the number of new customers.

Important to Break Down the Benefits

Usually, the most challenging part of the benefit map is establishing the cause-and-effect relationship between the benefits. In most cases, you will see that end benefits will be derived by improving performance (performance benefits). In the Nykredit case study, the driver behind revenue growth is an increase in the number of customers. It could also be a process improvement (performance benefit) that drives a reduced need for employees (end benefit), causing a financial saving (end benefit). The cause-and-effect logic does not consist of a fixed number of steps. The number of steps will depend on the complexity of the project. The important thing is that the benefits are broken down so that the performance benefits can be attributed directly to an employee group or department. At Nykredit, the 'New adviser team' is responsible for acquiring 270 customers and 'Other corporate advisers' are responsible for maturing existing customers.

Suppose we are not able to link performance benefits to specific employee groups. In that case, we are not able to have a conversation about the significance of the change, and how it affects the individual employee. That dialogue is key to understanding the project. After all, the project is intended to ensure that behavioural change occurs so the organisation can reap the benefits of the new behaviour.

Benefits Must Be Specific

The first time we work with the benefit map, we are often not aware of the size of the benefits. Instead, we work with rough benefit estimates or benefit hypotheses. In the Nykredit Business Bank case, we started out with a hypothesis of having DKK 5 million in total end benefits. Perhaps the amount turns out to be DKK 4 or 7 million, but having a starting point indicating a range will help us discuss which performance benefits are required, i.e. the number of customers. Annual revenue growth of DKK 5 million would require approximately 250 new customers per year, not 50 or 1000 new customers per year. Knowing this number at the first workshop enables us to have a productive discussion about the effect the project will have on the employees' work in the future. We use this knowledge to become more specific when outlining the new behaviour we need to achieve our goals.

Behaviour Versus Competencies

Once we have outlined the benefits and the new behaviour required to realise the benefits, the next step is to define the deliverables and activities needed for our colleagues to acquire the desired behaviour. Here we need to answer the last three questions to complete the benefit map:

1. What kind of support do our colleagues need in order to change their behaviour?
2. What kind of competencies are necessary for our colleagues to change their behaviour?
3. What kind of technical deliverables are required for our colleagues to change their behaviour?

Behaviour and competencies are defined for each group of employees. The behaviour column in Figure 4.3 contains specific behaviours, and the competencies column contains the *new* competencies a particular group of employees needs to attain. The big difference between competencies and behaviour is that, when you have the competency, you can, in principle, also act differently. The keyword here is 'can', as the fact that you are 'able to' is not the same as doing it. Sending your colleagues on a course to give them the necessary competencies is often not enough. Getting your colleagues to change their behaviour is a much bigger task.

The deliverables are placed furthest to the left and divided into three groups: technical, training, and change. Technical deliverables are classic deliverables such as an IT system, a process, or a product. Figure 4.5 illustrates that training deliverables support acquiring the competencies that each group of employees need. And change deliverables include the change support needed to achieve behavioural change among the groups of employees in question.

Since most of us come from a world where technical deliverables have been prevalent, they often take up more space than necessary. The benefit map's cause-and-effect relationships help identify which technical deliverables are crucial to value creation. If somebody wants to include technical deliverables that are not linked to the main benefits, they must have a very good reason to include them in the project's scope.

Box 4.1 The benefit map as a dialogue tool

The benefit map opens up a conversation about the following:

- What benefits the project needs to realise.
- How the organisation contributes to realising the benefits.
- The magnitude of the changes being introduced to the groups of employees in question.
- How small the technical scope can be and still deliver the most important benefits.
- The full set of prerequisites for how to create value with the project.

Figure 4.5 Training and change deliverables.

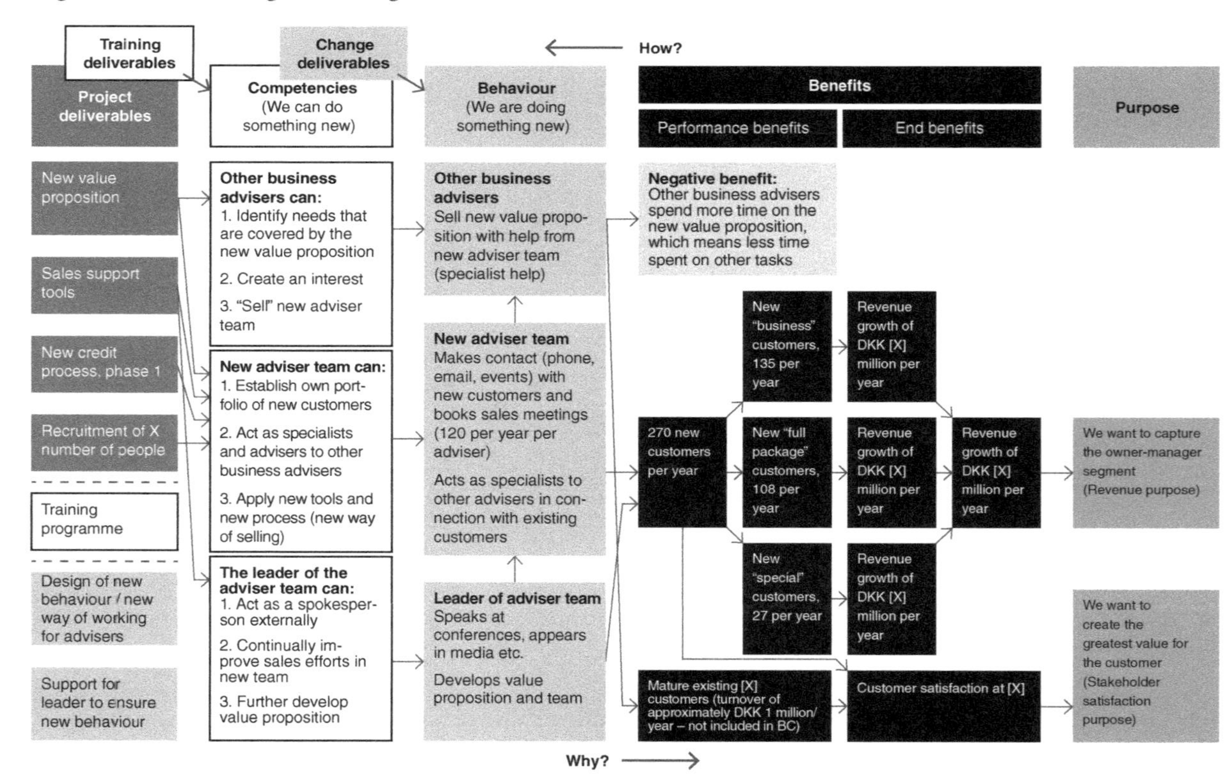

Using the benefit map as a dialogue tool, as outlined in Box 4.1, early in the project ensures that the steering committee establishes what benefits the project should deliver and how to realise them. In most cases, having conversations like these early on in the project saves the steering committee and the project group a considerable amount of time later on.

The Benefits Realisation Workshop Creates Ownership

The key to a successful project is to have the steering committee members participate in the benefits realisation workshop. The effect is lost if only people from the project group participate. They do not have the mandate to take responsibility and ownership for the project's benefits and the change required.

Before the benefits realisation method has become an integral part of our way of working, it may take a little tenacity and legwork to get the steering committee together for a three-hour workshop. But the effort is worth it. The benefits realisation workshop is a validation of benefit ownership and thus validation of the project's viability. However, the workshop will be cut short if we cannot find any benefit owners among the steering committee members. In that case, both the workshop and the project will be paused – at least until other potential benefit owners come forward. Without a clear managerial responsibility for the benefits, we cannot allow a project to proceed after the benefits realisation workshop.

From a benefit owner's perspective, the workshop is an excellent opportunity to shape the project and the expected benefits, ensuring that they end with the required project. In that way, ownership is not forced on the benefit owners, since they have been a part of outlining the project.

Define the Change

The next topic on the agenda is the change itself. At the benefits realisation workshop, we will have the first important conversation about the change necessary to realise the benefits. It is the first and most important step to successful change. The dialogue about what change each part of the organisation must go through to realise the benefits validates whether the benefit owners are willing to invest what is needed in their organisation.

In most organisations, the cost of change is both hidden and underestimated. The time the business spends implementing the change is often not included in the project's budget. Furthermore, we often assume that our colleagues will do their part once they have received training.

To question that assumption, we may ask the following questions:

- Do we know of a product that our sales department has not been able to sell?
- Have we at some point launched an IT system that has not been used to the extent that we intended?

The purpose of the questions is to discuss the individual employee groups' current behaviour and what it takes to change each group's behaviour. This conversation should give us an overall picture of what it will take to make the change happen and thus ensure that the benefit owners take ownership of both the benefits and the change.

If we succeed in creating ownership of both the benefits and the change needed to realise the benefits, we have done our best to ensure that the project becomes a success. This highlights the need to invest time in all three project tracks (benefit track, change track, and technical track) and do what is necessary to succeed.

> The benefits realisation workshop ensures that the benefit owners take ownership of the benefits and the change because they are the ones who design the project.

Who Should Attend the Workshop?

In addition to the steering committee, the project manager, and possibly a benefit specialist who contributes to facilitating the workshop, other specialists, or people from the project group, can also participate. During the benefits realisation workshop, the most important thing is to have the people present who are capable and have the mandate to design the project. In practice, it is not easy to get more than seven or eight participants to contribute actively during the workshop. Therefore, besides the steering committee, the number of participants should be adjusted to avoid stealing the focus from ensuring ownership and defining the project's direction.

The completion of the benefits realisation workshop is the kick-off for the rest of the project work in the analysis phase. In the many organisations that did not manage to fully integrate the benefits realisation method into their ways of working with projects, that kick-off is both the beginning and the end of the work with benefits realisation. A fantastic workshop is followed by returning to our old and familiar ways of working with projects. This means that we do not get the opportunity to lead the project with maximising benefits realisation as the guiding star. Consequently, we cannot prioritise or follow up on benefits and changes in behaviour at the portfolio level. Conducting the benefits realisation workshop is the first step on the maturity ladder and is summarised in Box 4.2. The next step is to clarify and quantify all parts of the benefit map during the analysis phase.

Box 4.2 Facilitating the benefits realisation workshop: a practical guide

Successful facilitation of the benefits realisation workshop is the ultimate test of a benefit specialist's abilities. The task can be compared to other ways of breaking down goals. The task is easy to understand, but it requires practice to become good at it.

The desired outcome of the workshop

- Develop the first version of the benefit map for the project on coloured index cards/Post-it notes to form the basis for further work on designing the project.

Before the workshop

There are several tasks to be addressed before the workshop:

1. Identifying (and, if necessary, motivating) the benefit owners and the rest of the steering committee.
2. Ensuring that the purpose is defined (see Chapter 1).
3. Preparing a facilitated session.

The most challenging facilitation task is to clarify the cause-and-effect relationships of the benefits. Therefore, as a facilitator, you should discuss what the breakdown of benefits could look like with a benefit owner or project participant. In that way, you avoid having to facilitate the workshop and get good ideas for the benefit cause-and-effect structure at the same time during the workshop. If necessary, sketch the entire benefit map as your own preparation for the workshop.

(*Continued*)

(Continued)

1. Book a venue with plenty of wall space for the benefit map. Alternatively, find a suitable virtual platform such as Miro.

During the workshop

A standard agenda for the benefits realisation workshop looks like this:

- Welcome, purpose, agenda, and a brief introduction to the project (10 minutes).
- A brief introduction to the benefits realisation tool and an example of the workshop's result (if the tool is not known in advance) (5–10 minutes).
- Workshop (2½ hours).
- Recap and next steps (5–10 minutes).

The workshop's point of departure is simple. We start by summarising and agreeing on the purpose and then roll out the cause-and-effect relationship from right to left, i.e. by answering the following questions:

- What is the purpose of the project?
  If the purpose is already defined, hang it on the wall from the beginning. Alternatively, you should formulate the desired value of the project and wait with the detailed wording until later.
- What benefits should be realised to fulfil our purpose?
  Take a starting point in one of the project's purposes, for example, revenue growth as in the Nykredit case

study in Figure 4.4. Define the end benefits (DKK X million in revenue per year) and break them down into performance benefits (270 new customers per year). Move on to the next purpose, define the end benefits, and break it down into performance benefits.
Note: for all benefits we expect to be measurable, we need to give an initial (nonbinding) estimate on the size of the end benefits and then on the performance benefits. Otherwise, we cannot have a conversation about how new performance goals affect each of the individual employee groups that need to change their ways of working.

- What new behaviour do our colleagues need to attain to realise our desired benefits?
  Go through all employee groups affected by the change and make the link to the performance benefits that each employee group must deliver. Discuss the size of the change for each employee group, for example based on T-shirt sizes (S, M, L, XL). In case there is a disagreement about the size of the change for a particular group of employees, we need to continue the dialogue until the steering committee has the same understanding of the change.
- What competencies are necessary for our colleagues to change their behaviour?
  For each group of employees, the *new* competencies the desired change requires are defined.
- What deliverables are necessary for our colleagues to attain the new behaviour?

(*Continued*)

(Continued)

For each employee group, the following is defined: what technical deliverables are needed, what training deliverables are needed to meet the competency requirements, and what change deliverables will help this group of employees change their behaviour.

How do we create value as quickly as possible?

- What launch options, i.e. combinations of technical, training, and change deliverables, help us realise some of the benefits as quickly as possible? The launch strategies are reviewed in Chapter 7.
- What series of launches could the project consist of?

When the benefit map is completed, the next step is to determine when the steering committee will be involved again – to clarify outstanding issues or see the next version of the benefit map and the analyses behind this version.

After the workshop

The benefit map is documented and kept up to date throughout the project.

Practical deviations

If you follow the agenda, you will get the answers to the questions in the right order. Thus, you will have a good starting point for completing the project design at the end of the workshop. In practice, situations will arise where it makes sense to change the order of the questions or skip steps to have time for the most important conversations if time is short.

Generally, the most important conversations during the workshop are those about benefits and new behaviour. So, if time is running short, this is where the focus should be. The second priority is the technical deliverables, especially what is key to realising the most important benefits. When you start deviating from the fixed structure but still manage to make time for the most important conversations about design, you have become an experienced facilitator of the benefit map.

Cause-and-effect deviations

The benefit map is designed for change projects. Suppose the project's purpose is to replace a server that improves response times for an IT system or provides lower operating costs. In that case, there will be an arrow from the technical deliverable 'Replacement of server' to the benefit 'X% faster response time'.

If the behavioural change requires us to stop doing something, for example providing a particular service to our colleagues, the new behaviour is not dependent on new competencies or technical deliverables. On the other hand, it often requires considerable change efforts, as resistance can easily arise when we ask an employee group to reduce the level of service to colleagues, customers or citizens.

From the example in Figure 4.6, you can see the headings from the benefits realisation process at the top, and below them, the project is unfolded. Note that the cause-and-effect relationship is shown by placing the coloured index cards in continuation with each other.

(*Continued*)

(Continued)

Format	Workshop (physical or virtual)
Materials	Coloured index cards (like in Figure 4.6) or large Post-it notes if the workshop takes place physically
Duration	Typically 2½ to 3 hours
Participants	Benefit owners, other steering committee members, project managers, possibly a benefit specialist, project participants, or subject matter experts
Result	The first version of the benefit map on coloured index cards/Post-it notes

Figure 4.6 Example of a benefit map after the first workshop.

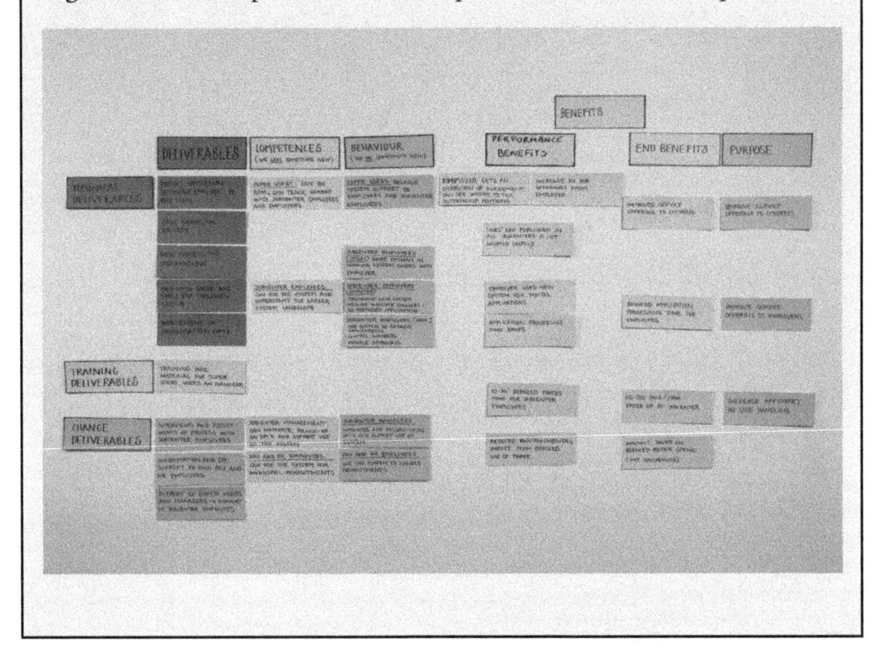

5

The Benefit Track in the Analysis Phase

The first step of the project has now been completed. Together with the steering committee, a benefit-driven project design has been made, resulting in the first version of the benefit map. So far, so good.

The next part of the analysis phase is divided into the benefit track, change track, and technical track. In this chapter, I will go through the benefit track. The key to detailing the benefit and change part of the benefit map is to make it simple. During the analysis phase, the task is to estimate the benefits and describe at what pace we expect them to be realised. Thus, at the end of the analysis phase, we have a benefits realisation plan that shows when the project is expected to realise its benefits.

Before we estimate IT deliverables, efforts to create organisational change, and benefits, we need to consider how the estimates will be used. The time we spend on estimation must be weighed against the type and importance of the decisions estimates are going to support. If we decide to work three months on the project and then reprioritise based on our new learnings, estimates with less certainty can be sufficient compared to a situation where we must decide once and for all whether to carry out a big project. The accuracy of the estimates should be similar for the cost of technical deliverables, the organisational change, and the benefits, as we will weigh them against each other to assess the project. In any case, the quality of the benefit estimates should be of such quality that it will allow the benefit owner to take ownership of the benefits realisation. Figure 5.1 highlights the benefit track in the analysis phase.

The process of estimating benefits consists of five steps. The first step is the benefits realisation workshop. Here the steering committee outlines the project's cause-and-effect structure and thus the prerequisites for how the benefits are realised (1). The next steps focus on validating the cause-and-effect relationships of the benefits (2), establishing a baseline (3), and estimating the benefits (4). The organisations used to working with business cases can use part of that experience in this process. The main thing is to create a clear cause-and-effect relationship between the end benefits and the new behaviour we need to attain. Before that is done, we are not able to define the new behaviour, and thus we are unable to set the scope of the project.

The analysis work in the benefit track and change track is therefore closely linked. The estimation of benefits cannot be completed without confirming that the change in behaviour, which is the prerequisite for realising the benefits, is also possible with a change effort that fits within the project's budget. The final step is the steering committee's approval of the completed benefit map, including input from the technical track and change track (5).

The process is rarely linear. There will often be rework, and in large-scale projects, it is usually necessary to get the steering committee's input several times.

Figure 5.1 The benefit track in the analysis phase.

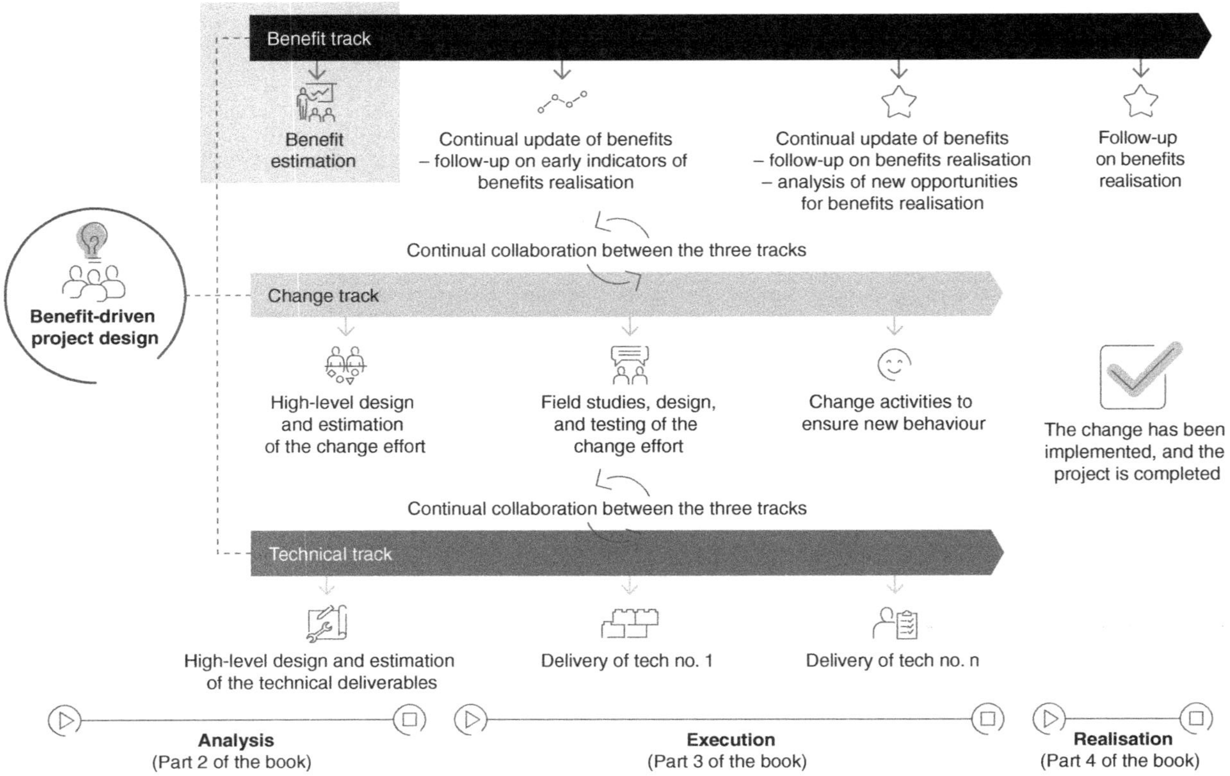

Estimating Benefits

The steps where we establish the baseline and estimate the benefits are usually the most time-consuming parts of the process. The five steps to estimate benefits are outlined in Figure 5.2.

Consider the following before choosing estimation methods:

- Which method or combination of methods will provide the most accurate estimates?
- What is the method's cost of collecting data compared to other methods?

In Figure 5.3, I briefly describe the methods that can be used in the project.

Internal data will often be available when optimising processes, but if not, it will often be possible to make simulations to help us estimate what improvements we can expect. The simulation method may also involve putting new products up for sale on the company's website and seeing if someone presses 'purchase'. In case of higher uncertainty, the need to lean on several types of methods for estimating benefits often increases, for example benchmarking and reference cases. If there is not enough help from any of the first four methods, you may need to make a pilot project and assess its viability, as was the case for Nykredit Business Bank.

The Benefit Owner Must Be Able to Vouch for the Estimate

The benefits are usually estimated by employees from the benefit owner's organisation, as this is often where the necessary knowledge is present. The benefit owner must own the estimates entirely. Therefore, the project manager and benefit specialists can never become more than a support function in the estimation efforts.

Figure 5.2 Five-step benefit estimation.

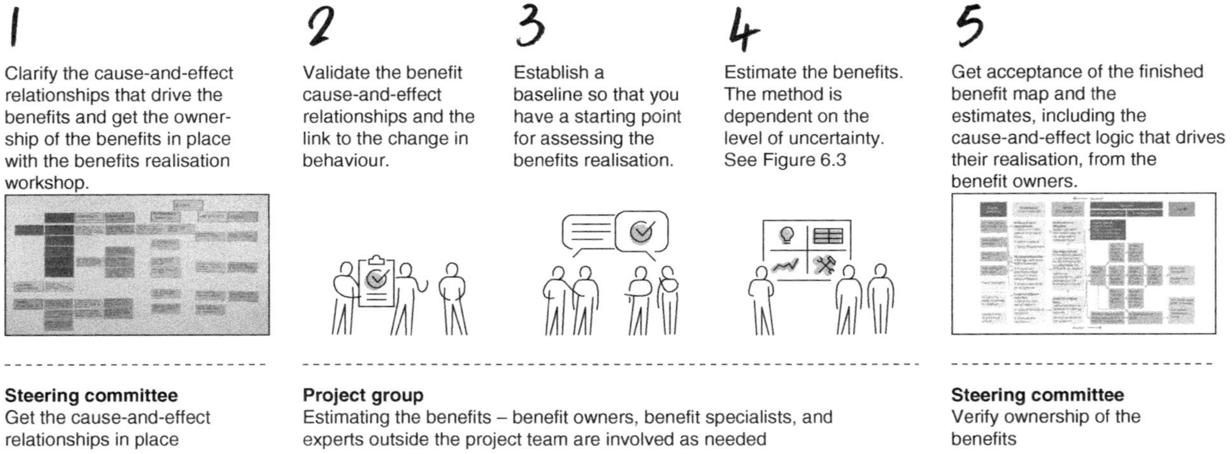

Figure 5.3 Methods for estimating benefits.

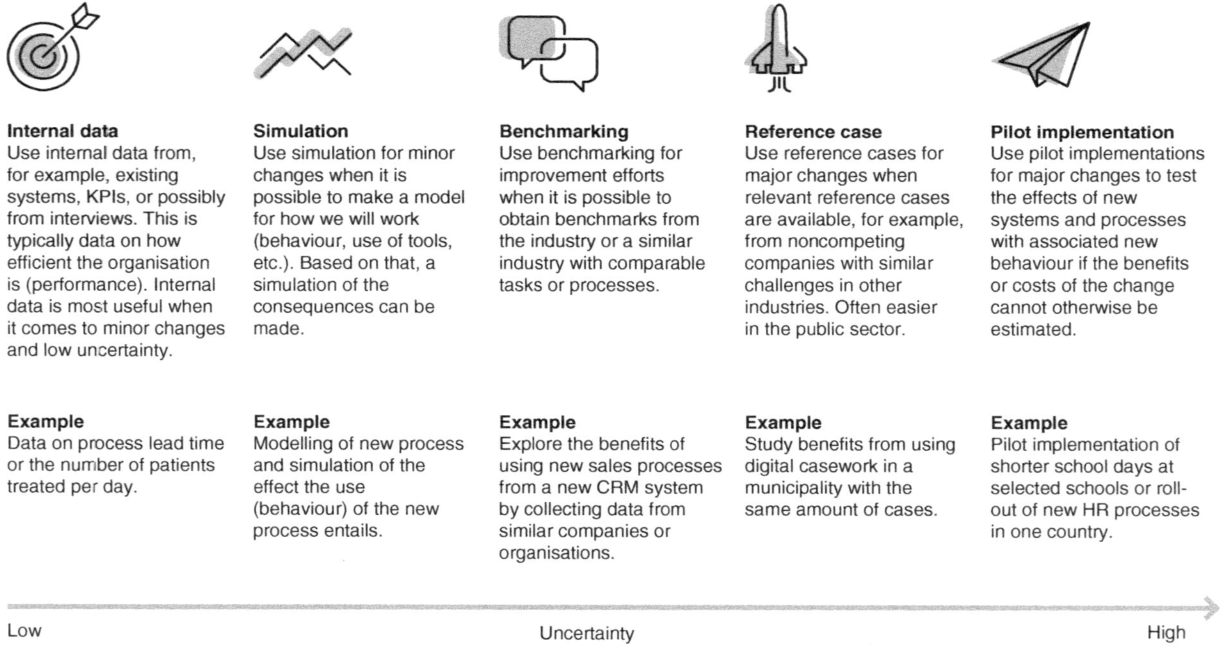

Internal data
Use internal data from, for example, existing systems, KPIs, or possibly from interviews. This is typically data on how efficient the organisation is (performance). Internal data is most useful when it comes to minor changes and low uncertainty.

Example
Data on process lead time or the number of patients treated per day.

Simulation
Use simulation for minor changes when it is possible to make a model for how we will work (behaviour, use of tools, etc.). Based on that, a simulation of the consequences can be made.

Example
Modelling of new process and simulation of the effect the use (behaviour) of the new process entails.

Benchmarking
Use benchmarking for improvement efforts when it is possible to obtain benchmarks from the industry or a similar industry with comparable tasks or processes.

Example
Explore the benefits of using new sales processes from a new CRM system by collecting data from similar companies or organisations.

Reference case
Use reference cases for major changes when relevant reference cases are available, for example, from noncompeting companies with similar challenges in other industries. Often easier in the public sector.

Example
Study benefits from using digital casework in a municipality with the same amount of cases.

Pilot implementation
Use pilot implementations for major changes to test the effects of new systems and processes with associated new behaviour if the benefits or costs of the change cannot otherwise be estimated.

Example
Pilot implementation of shorter school days at selected schools or roll-out of new HR processes in one country.

Low — Uncertainty — High

Source: Inspired by Ward and Daniel (2012).
CRM – customer relationship management; KPI – key performance indicator.

Responsibility for the benefits and the knowledge they are based on must come from the benefit owner and their organisation. If there is a lot of uncertainty associated with the estimates, a pragmatic solution is to multiply an uncertainty factor on the estimates or estimate the benefits within a range. The benefit owners can then take ownership of realising the benefits in the low end of the range. However, a possible consequence is that a business case with fewer benefits could lead to the project not being prioritised.

Box 5.1 unfolds the five benefit estimation steps in the Nykredit pilot project.

Box 5.1 Estimating benefits in the Nykredit Business Bank pilot project

As mentioned in Chapters 3 and 4, Nykredit had decided to pursue the owner-manager segment. However, the venture was subject to considerable uncertainty as it was difficult to estimate precisely how many new customers the initiative would attract. Therefore, Nykredit chose to carry out Project White Coats, a pilot project on their Business Bank initiative. The project's results would decide whether or not to introduce Nykredit Business Bank to the whole owner-manager segment.

Listed below are the activities in each step in Project White Coats.

1. The benefits were structured in a benefit map at the benefits realisation workshop.
2. Internal experts validated the benefits' cause-and-effect relationships.

(Continued)

(Continued)

3. A baseline was established. Since any additional revenue would be generated by new customers because there was no real influx of customers in the White Coats segment, the baseline for customer and revenue growth was zero.
4. The benefit estimates were based on external data on segment size, internal data on current revenue of White Coats customers, and educated guesses about how to focus their sales efforts to get new customers. No good benchmark or reference data was available for the relationship between the sales efforts needed to get one new customer for that segment. Benefit data was linked to adviser behaviour by making assumptions (guesses) about how many customer contacts (emails, phone calls, meetings at events) it would take to get a sales meeting with a customer and the conversion rate between sales meetings and new customers.
5. The steering committee presented and approved the final benefit map, supported by a benefits realisation plan and additional material on the background of the established benefit assumptions. In the process, Vice President Carsten Kruse, the project's benefit owner, had been involved and participated in discussions about the benefits' assumptions to be able to vouch for estimates and own the end benefits.

The first time we measure how far we have come in the benefits realisation process, we have often only achieved a fraction of the desired result. In many cases, benefits realisation increases over a period of time until it is fully phased in. Therefore, the result of the estimation effort should give us estimates on the end goal and the expected phase-in so that it becomes possible to see if we are on the right track. To do so, we use the benefits realisation plan.

The Benefits Realisation Plan

To ensure that both the project's execution and realisation phases realise as many benefits as possible, we use the benefits realisation plan to follow up on the project's benefits realisation.

The plan contains KPIs for the most important leading indicators of benefits realisation (developing new competencies and new behaviour) and the benefits. The leading indicators originate from the change track and include developing competencies and new behaviour. Setting targets for early indicators is equal to defining end-state ambitions and setting milestones to achieve them for deliverables in the technical track. Early indicators ensure that we have the same opportunities to follow up on the change track that we have in the technical track. Both leading indicators and benefits are broken down over time, making it clear whether we are on the right track to reach our early indicator and benefit targets.

Developing KPIs

The number of KPIs we select to track the project's benefits realisation must be weighed against the effort required to continually provide data for them. It is therefore important to identify the 'benefits realisation highway' through the project. This 'highway' consists of the benefits, the changed behaviour, and the most critical competencies and deliverables that are the most important for value creation and, therefore, the ones we follow up on. Finding the right number of KPIs for the project to follow up on is a balancing act. On the one hand, the KPIs put focus on realising the benefits, but on the other hand, there is a cost of collecting data and a limit on how much data we are able to follow up on at portfolio level. A small-scale project, such as the Nykredit Business Bank pilot, should only have one highway of KPIs.

The benefits realisation highway is illustrated in Figure 5.4. The individual KPIs must also appear in the benefits realisation plan where the highway's KPIs are shown over time. In that way, it will be possible to see whether the project realises its benefits during its execution and after it is completed.

Table 5.1 shows the front page of the benefits realisation plan for the Nykredit Business Bank pilot. The KPIs are the same as those constituting the benefits realisation highway in Figure 5.4, except for the deliverables. To be able to continually follow up, it is necessary to break down the benefits we track in periods of, for example, three or six months. This is done to make it possible to adjust our efforts in the project or start new initiatives on an ongoing basis if we at some point in time have failed to realise the expected benefits.

Large-scale Projects

In projects that are more extensive than the Nykredit Business Bank pilot, there are often ongoing launches, potentially from several highways, creating different types of benefits, such as revenue or costs. 'Launch' is understood as a combination of activities and deliverables from the technical track and change track, respectively, that create the basis for benefits realisation. The strategy for the number, content, and timing of the launches naturally influences costs and how quickly we reap the benefits in the business case.

If the project has more than one launch, we start tracking benefits after the first launch. At that point, we will also follow up on technical deliverables and leading change indicators for the

Figure 5.4 The benefits realisation highway.

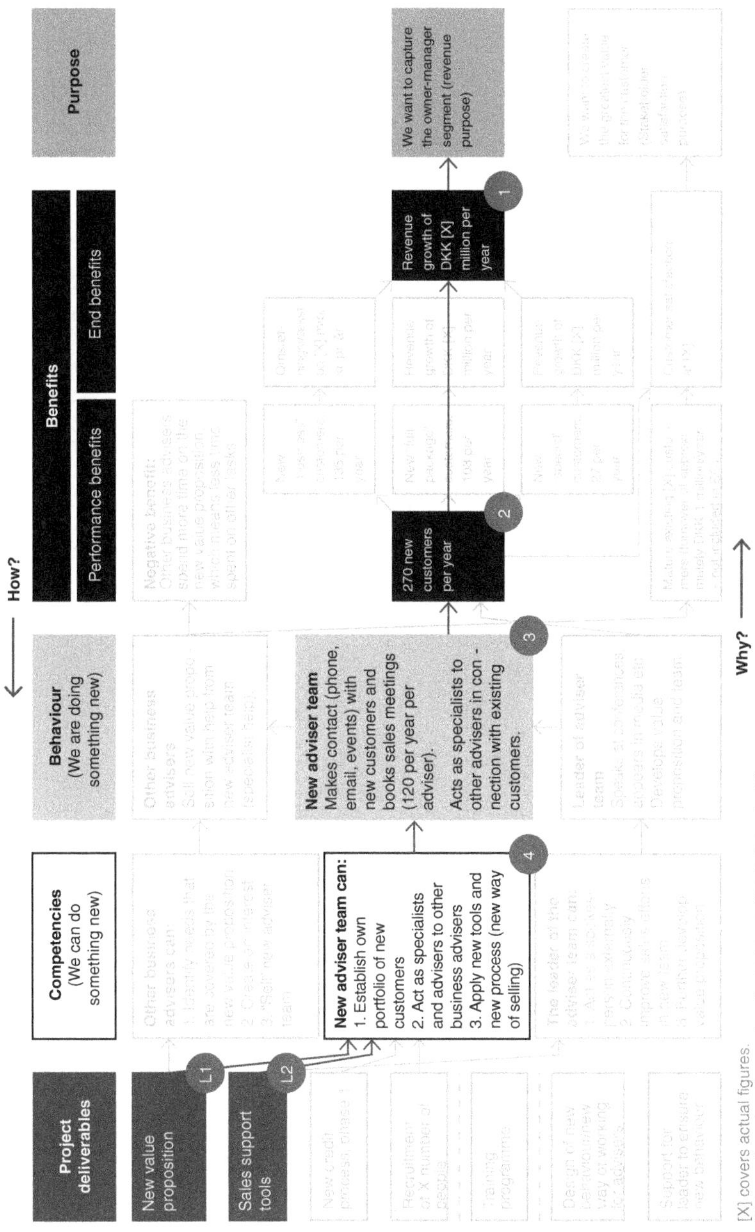

[X] covers actual figures.
The number of customers is adjusted according to the actual figures

Table 5.1 Benefits realisation plan for the Nykredit Business Bank pilot: baseline and overview of end goals.

Benefits and early indicators of benefit realisation				**Project period**	
No.	**Benefit/early indicator of benefit realisation**	**Measurement**	**Owner**	**Baseline (year 0)**	**End target**
End benefits					
1	Revenue growth from new customers in the “White coats” segment	CRM system report	Carsten Kruse (Vice President)	DKK 0 (almost no customer growth)	DKK X million in increased revenue after three years
Performance improvements					
2	New customers in the “White coats” segment	CRM system report	Carsten Kruse (Vice President)	0 new customers	810 new customers after three years
Behaviour					
3	Advisers in “new adviser team” conduct direct selling and use new sales process	Observations, conversations and CRM system report	Marianne (teamleder)	0% conduct sales as agreed	100% conduct sales as agreed
Competencies					
4	Advisers are trained specialists in the “White coats” segment, the new sales process and the new value proposition	Four case tests during training	Sofie (project manager)	0% have passed case tests	100% have passed case tests

parts of the project that are still being implemented. However, this does not change the format of the benefits realisation plan. It just becomes more extensive. The consequences of the delivery strategy on the work in the benefit track are discussed in Part 3 of the book on the execution of the project. Furthermore, the use of data from the benefits realisation plan to the prioritisation of the portfolio is discussed in Part 4, on the portfolio management office's (PMO) role in scaling the benefits realisation method to all projects in the organisation.

The Benefit Part of the Business Case

Once the benefit map and the benefits realisation plan are completed in the analysis phase, we are very close to having the inputs we need to create the benefit part of the business case.

The benefit map shows the content of the project we assume will realise the end benefits, and the benefits realisation plan shows when we expect to realise them. Now we only need to determine what benefits we can hold a benefit owner accountable for. Two criteria must be met to determine this. The project's benefits must be quantifiable and traceable. In theory, there are very few benefits that cannot be quantified. In practice, however, it can be expensive or require us to disturb many employees, customers, or citizens to quantify some of the benefits.

Traceable and Nontraceable Benefits

If we identify a benefit as 'Reduced risk of bankruptcy due to lack of innovation', we must show it. However, if we are unable to create a baseline or measure it, we cannot hold a benefit owner accountable for it either. Quantifiable benefits are divided into two categories: traceable and nontraceable benefits.

It is often easier to trace the benefits in projects where we only depend on colleagues in our own organisation. Here, the cause-and-effect relationships in the benefit map are usually certain. Therefore, it is also reasonable to hold the benefit owners accountable for the result. If we do a process optimisation project, we are responsible for ensuring that the processes are followed (behaviour), and improved performance and time saved take place in our own organisation. If time saved is to be used for financial savings in the form of reduced payroll costs or for solving other tasks, we have the opportunity to manage it.

Traceability can be somewhat more difficult to establish when we aim to realise benefits that depend on the behaviour of customers, citizens, suppliers, or others outside our organisation. If more people come to the libraries, was it because of our project or because other cultural activities nearby closed or because the local schools introduced a weekly library visit for the pupils? If sales in Germany exceed our expectations, how much did each of the four promotional projects contribute? Perhaps sales have simply gone up because one of our competitors has been involved in a corruption scandal? To place ownership of a benefit, it must be traceable to the individual project, and it must be possible to quantify the benefit.

Figure 5.5 illustrates that a benefit owner can only be accountable for the benefits in the upper right square.

Include All Benefits in the Final Assessment

Although there are challenges in quantifying the benefits, they must still appear in the benefit map if we believe they are there. Suppose there are issues with traceability or quantifiability. In that case, we cannot hold a benefit owner accountable for them, and therefore we cannot include them in the financial part of the business case either. In some cases, traceability issues can be

Figure 5.5 The benefit owner's accountability for the benefits.

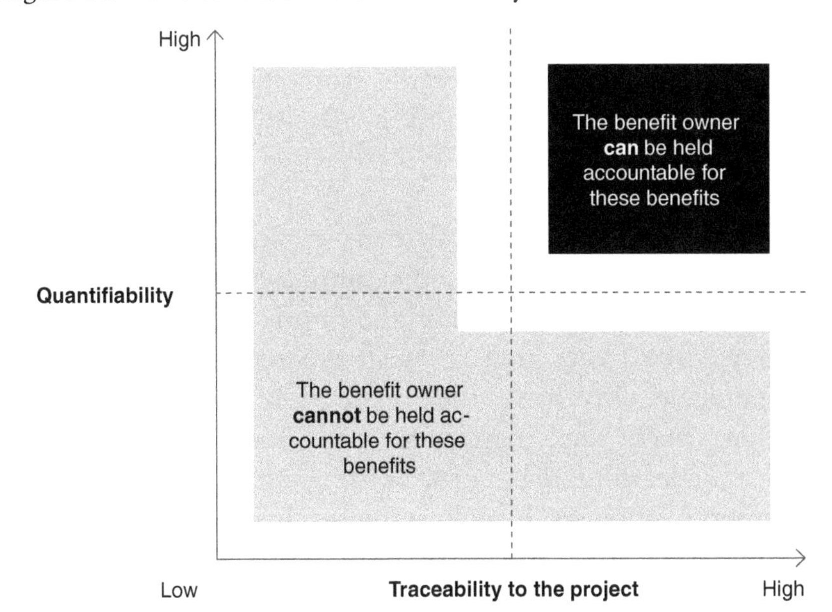

solved by gathering a number of projects aimed at realising the same benefits in a programme where benefit ownership stretches across individual projects. In other cases, we must backtrack along the benefits realisation highway until we find traceable and quantifiable benefits.

In the last instance, we might need to settle for placing responsibility and following up on the behavioural changes in our organisation since that is something for which we can always assign accountability. Benefits characterised by a low level of quantifiability or traceability, or both, should be included in the overall assessment of the project's success – even if they cannot be included in the financial part of the project's business case. The assessment of whether the business case is good becomes more subjective in those situations, as we weigh quantifiable costs against benefits for which we cannot reasonably place ownership.

Remember the Indirect Benefits

The benefits attributed directly from the project to the organisation's bottom line often get the most attention. However, this does not signify that they are the only benefits worth focusing on.

I have previously stated that many projects also generate indirect benefits, i.e. benefits that improve the organisation's ability to make change happen in the future. The indirect benefits are typically greatest in large-scale projects or projects where, for example, we also change the organisation's ability to carry out future projects by applying new methods. Here we can consider whether the learning that a project brings should be included as a benefit and supported by deliverables to strengthen and sustain it. In most projects, however, the indirect benefits are small and of lesser importance.

In the Nykredit Business Bank example, the benefits realisation method was used for the first time in Nykredit. The approach provided learnings on working with benefits realisation, which was incorporated as a new method and used in subsequent projects. The introduction of the benefits realisation method is an indirect benefit of the Nykredit Business Bank project, which is not shown in the benefit map. Partly because it was not part of the project's purpose and partly because, at the time, we did not realise what leverage the benefits realisation method would get from the project.

6

The Change Track in the Analysis Phase

The change track brings together the tasks that are about making change happen. The purpose is to ensure that all employees who will be affected by the change get through the process in a good and efficient way, enabling us to create the new behaviour required to unlock the full potential of the benefits.

In line with the benefit track, the change track is divided into an analysis phase and execution phase (Figure 6.1). In the analysis phase, called the change analysis, we learn more about the extent of the change and how to achieve it successfully. In the execution phase, we will ensure that this happens.

The change analysis starts right after the benefits realisation workshop.

For the change track, the trick is to regard the change just as you would the technical aspect of the project. Similar to technical deliverables, it is essential to specify the change activities in order to estimate and plan them. Therefore, we must design and understand the many facets of the change before executing the project, just as we do in the technical track. In addition, we must create the best possible basis for the subsequent change efforts

Figure 6.1 The change track in the analysis phase: the change analysis.

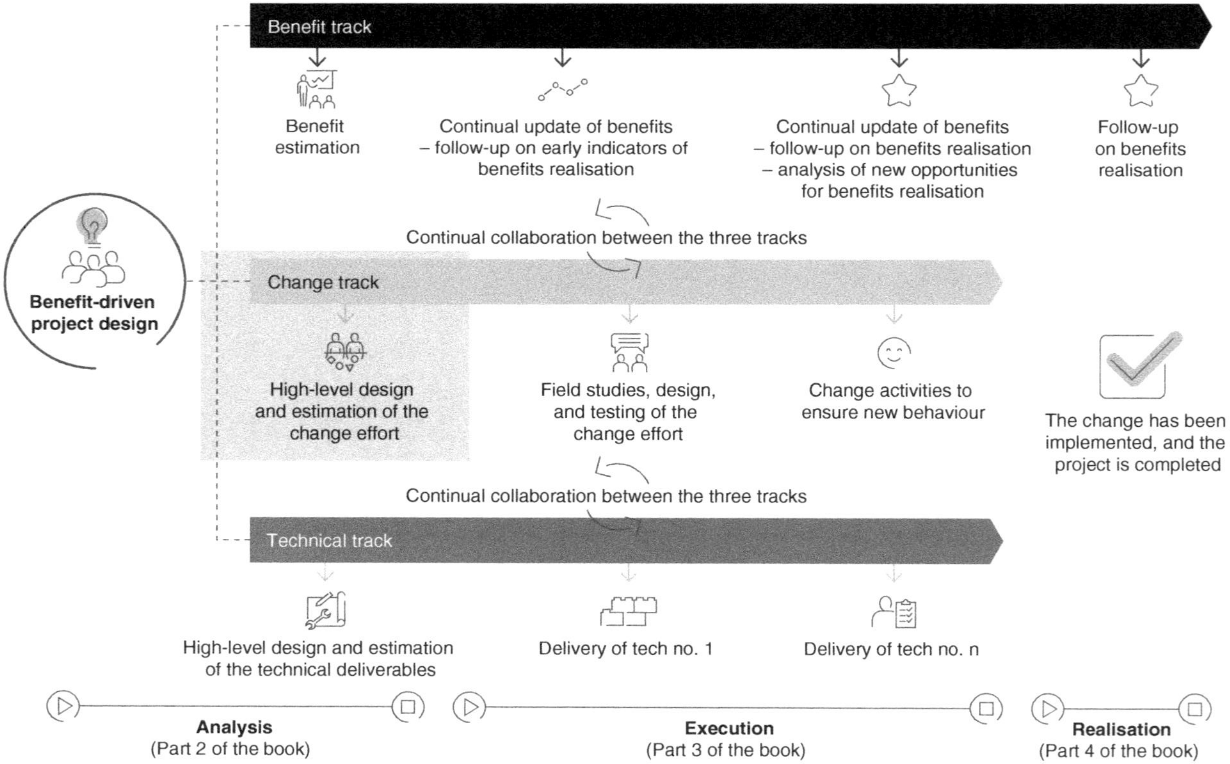

Figure 6.2 Change deliverables and goals of the analysis phase.

DELIVERABLES:
- Description of the expected new behaviour for each of the affected employee groups
- Overview of expected change activities
- Estimate of the change effort, including the efforts of the managers and the employee ambassadors involved
- Change plan
- Requirements for technical deliverables that create the prerequisites for new behaviour

CHANGE OBJECTIVES:
- Continued ownership of and demand for the change among the benefit owners
- Ownership of and demand for the change among the first-line managers and employee ambas - sadors involved in the analysis
- Room for the affected employees to make the change their own

by engaging and creating ownership among the managers and employees from the business who will be involved in the analysis phase.

In the analysis phase, we involve the managers of the employees who will be impacted most by the change, and the employees we expect can become excellent ambassadors when/if the project is completed. The change deliverables and goals of the analysis phase are summarised in Figure 6.2.

The benefits realisation workshop forms the basis for the change track. Here we sketch the project design by way of the benefit map, as shown in Figure 4.6. The map shows which groups of employees will be affected, details the expected new behaviour for each group, and indicates the size of the change and what new competencies each group of employees need to develop. However, there is very important work to be done after the benefits realisation workshop to achieve the objectives of the analysis phase.

Participants and the Content of the Change Analysis

The most important participants in the change analysis are the benefit owner and first-line manager, preferably flanked by a few employees who we expect to become ambassadors and play a significant role in the change efforts.

In smaller projects, the benefit owner and first-line manager are often one and the same. In larger projects, the benefit owner and first-line manager may be at different organisational levels. Here the change analysis ensures that we involve all relevant managers whose employees will be significantly affected by the change. The benefit owner's ownership of and support for the change efforts are key prerequisites for realising the benefits. Still, the most important player in making change happen is the first-line manager.[1]

Involving the First-line Manager

Suppose the first-line manager has helped design the project in the benefits realisation workshop. In that case, they are ready to participate in the change analysis and equip the employee ambassadors for their upcoming task. Alternatively, the benefit owner must introduce the first-line manager to the project. It is important to involve the first-line manager and a few future ambassadors. Their involvement gives us a much better picture of what is going on in the employee group and what is required to make the change happen. Employee involvement often enriches our knowledge of what is actually happening in the organisation, even more than we can learn from the first-line manager alone.

---

[1] Gottschalk et al. (2017). The study 'Change Management in IT Projects' was conducted by the Saïd Business School at the University of Oxford and by the Implement Consulting Group. It shows that the first-line manager's involvement is more important than other management layers.

Additionally, the first-line manager and ambassadors often provide new input for potential benefits and input on how to realise the benefits that have already been identified.

The number of people we choose to involve in the analysis phase is a delicate balancing act. On the one hand, we want to get an accurate estimate of new behaviour, the size of the change, and the efforts needed to implement the change. On the other hand, there are costs involved when involving many people and raising concerns about a change project that may never even see the light of day.

> As a rule of thumb, the manager and at least one employee who can act as a change ambassador should be involved from each department if the size of the change has been categorised as 'Medium', 'Large', or 'X-Large' at the benefits realisation workshop.

The Change Workshop Sets the Direction

Once the participants in the change analysis are mobilised, it is time for the main activity in the change analysis, namely the change workshop. Here, we design our first take on the new behaviour and the efforts that the change activities require for each group of affected employees.

After the change workshop, the person responsible for the change track, and possibly other people allocated to the change track, further details the workshop's output, possibly with input from the first-line manager and ambassadors involved. The result is a proposal for specific change activities, including resource estimates and plans that are then validated by the first-line manager of the employee group. The activities in the change analysis for each group of employees are shown in Figure 6.3, while Box 6.1 shows how to craft the project's story.

Figure 6.3 Change analysis activities by employee group.

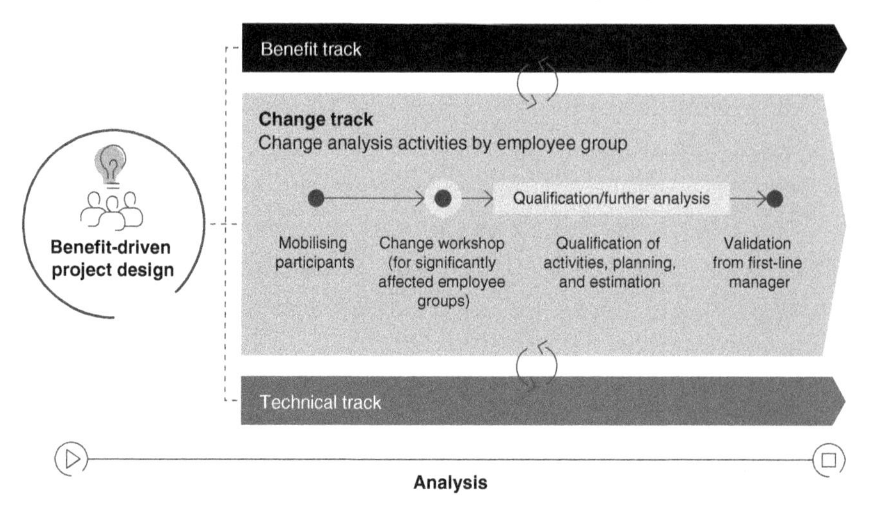

Box 6.1: The story of the project

A project's story is essential. Often, it is the first introduction an employee or manager gets to the project. If it is well orchestrated, it creates an awareness of the project's purpose and expected benefits. Why is it worth investing time in the project?

Communication in the form of stories about *why* and preferably also *how* the change will happen is a 'push activity' where we push information out into the organisation. The story about the project carries both the message of managerial support and the rationale behind the project. Both are a necessary foundation for us to start working on the change efforts.

Suppose we use the story only in a one-to-many relationship. In that case, it has some effect, for example a sanctioning of spending time on the project or the story

(*Continued*)

(Continued)

becoming an anchor point for future conversations about the project. Suppose we use the story in smaller forums to start a dialogue about how we locally contribute to realising benefits and thus achieve our purpose. In that case, the impact will be much greater. If we succeed in telling a story that conveys managerial support and creates curiosity, demand, and a positive emotional response, the story not only creates the prerequisite for working with behavioural change but also helps in making the change happen.

The first version of the story takes shape when we define the purpose of the project. Here we begin to structure the narrative of why the project is a good idea. The next version of the story comes after the benefits realisation workshop, as we then have a better picture of why we are doing the project and what it will take. When there is time to explain the details of the project, the benefit map is an excellent and effective communication tool. In other cases, there may be a need to formalise the story further. To help formulate the story, you can use the structured message framework (Figure 6.4). The framework creates a structure and a focus by dividing the story into:

- Key message.
- Supportive messages.
- Behaviour, themes, or facts supporting the messages.

The key message of the project is typically linked to the strategic purpose, while the supportive messages are linked to the project's purpose or end benefits. The messages are backed up by new behaviour or themes about what

(Continued)

(*Continued*)

Figure 6.4 The structured message framework.

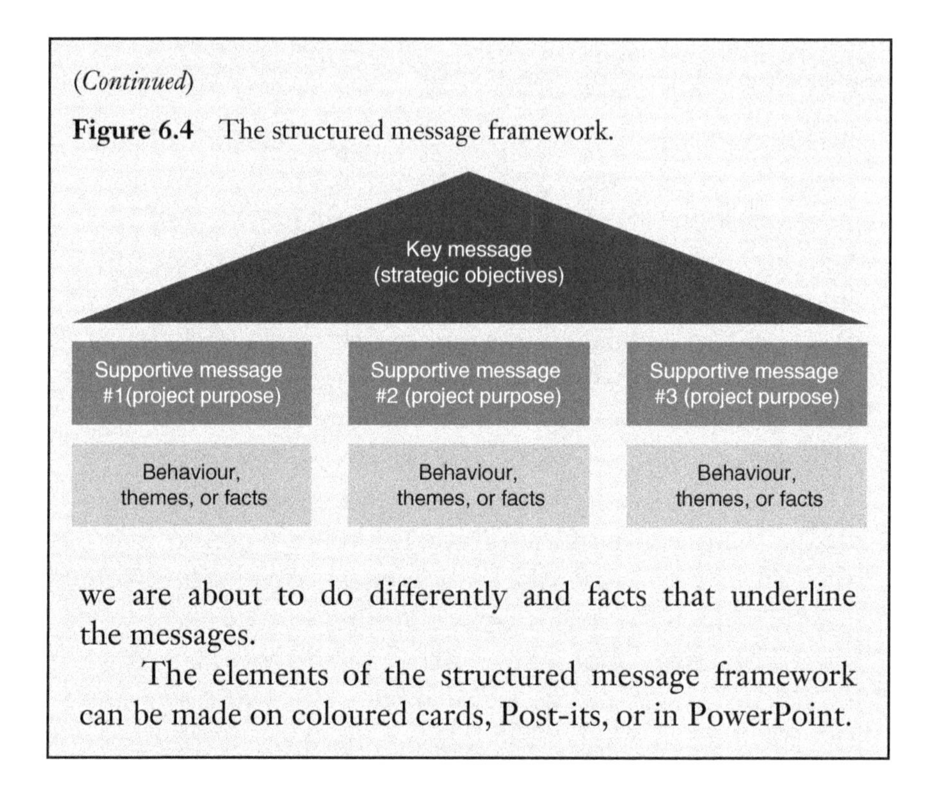

we are about to do differently and facts that underline the messages.

The elements of the structured message framework can be made on coloured cards, Post-its, or in PowerPoint.

Behavioural Change

We talk about the change at the benefits realisation workshop at employee group level. It gives an overview of which groups of employees will be affected by the change and how big we think it will be, and thus forms the basis for further analysis.

Since we need to understand the change and what it takes to make it happen in practice, we must look at what barriers the individual employee needs to overcome and understand the employee's behaviour as an interaction with the surroundings.

The barrier wheel illustrates the different types of barriers to change in Figure 6.5. At the centre are the individual and barriers they face. We have the organisational barriers on the left-hand side of the wheel, while the technical barriers are on the

Figure 6.5 The barrier wheel.

Organisational barriers

Groups

Is there anything in the group that works against new behaviour? For example, in language or conversations or in the attitude towards management? Are there groups in the group?

Organisational structure

Are there any factors in the organisation that counteract the desired behaviour? For example, in rules, values, incentives, resources, or organisational structure?

Norms and culture

Does the organisational culture and norms enable the desired behaviour, or are there organisational culture and norms that stand in the way of being able to create change?

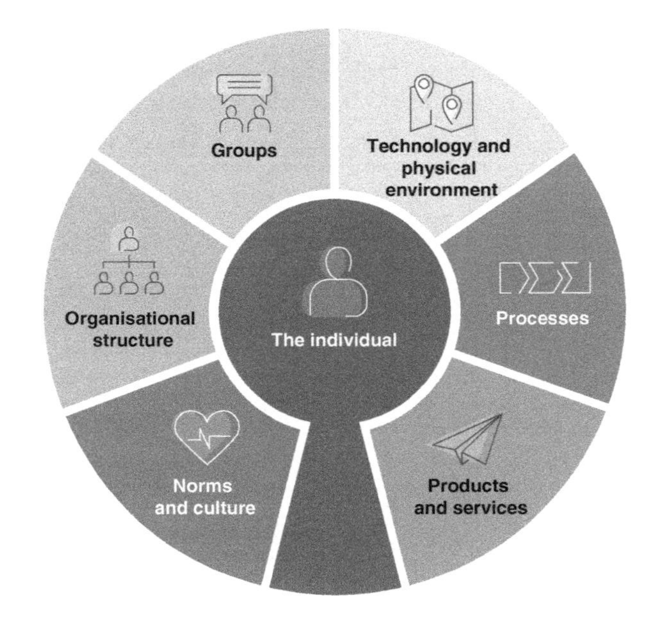

Individual barriers

What reactions to change can we anticipate in each employee, and how should we deal with them? What competencies create the prerequisites for the new behaviour?

Technical barriers

Technology and physical environment

Are the technological tools adequate and intuitive? Do they support or obstruct the desired behaviour? How do the office decor, lighting, etc., back up the current behaviour, and does it work for the new behaviour?

Processes

In what way is the current process related to behaviour? Do we need to change processes or procedures? What habits are currently an integrated part of our work life, and should we change them?

Products and services

What new products or services, if any, are necessary to enable the new behaviour?

Source: Designed by Mads Herskind and Rasmus Rytter with inspiration from Grech et al. (2008).

right-hand side. The barrier wheel forms the basis for our work to learn more about the change and what it takes to change behaviour.

The Roles of the Change Track and Technical Track

When the behaviour of our employees and colleagues is crucial to benefits realisation, the requirements for the project should originate from what it takes to get the individual employee to change their behaviour. The change analysis will articulate the need for the deliverables and activities we need to carry out in the change track. Furthermore, our need to overcome the technical barriers will translate into requirements for the technical deliverables, including IT and technology, physical environment, processes and business processes, and products and services. This does not mean it is a one-way communication of requirements from the change track to the technical track. The tasks in the two tracks are often deeply integrated, and especially in projects involving major technical implementations, there is a great deal of mutual influence between them. On the one hand, we have the demand from the change track, and on the other hand we have the technical track's inputs about what technical possibilities are available – and at what cost.

The key to the design of the overall project is to maintain the connection between the desired benefits, the behavioural change required, and the barriers the project must remove or circumvent to succeed. The change track and technical track are often closely linked in terms of staffing, as people from the business work in both tracks. As a general rule, the change track should map deliverables and activities, the cost and a plan for the new behaviour, competency building, and the deliverable to remove or circumvent the organisational barriers (for example new organisation design or incentive structure).

During the analysis, the technical track includes the requirements for the technical deliverables needed to ensure the new behaviour. The track incorporates them with any other requirements for the technical deliverables, for example requirements derived from an IT solution having to fit into the existing IT architecture. The technical track produces specifications, estimates, and plans for the execution of the technical deliverables with the level of detail required to decide whether the project should proceed after the analysis has been completed.

The Change Workshop

The change workshop is designed to help the first-line manager and a few future employee ambassadors to get all the way around the change step by step.

The first-line manager and the ambassadors must clarify what benefits we can realise, what change activities it takes for the particular group of employees, and what it takes to make the change happen. The workshop sets the direction for a subsequent clarification and analysis of the change efforts. The process helps create or reinforce the ownership of the change, which in itself becomes a decisive factor in the success of the change efforts.

The change workshop consists of four steps, as shown in Figure 6.6.

Before we dive into the change workshop, you will get a brief introduction to the sterilisation centre project from the University of Copenhagen. It provides an example of how the change workshop can be conducted and the outcome.

Case: University of Copenhagen's Sterilisation Centre

'In today's educational sector, it is crucial that we deliver results. The benefits realisation method helps us focus on the results of our projects and ensures that we achieve them.'

Anders V. Møller, Faculty Director (2016–19),
University of Copenhagen

Figure 6.6 Content of the change workshop.

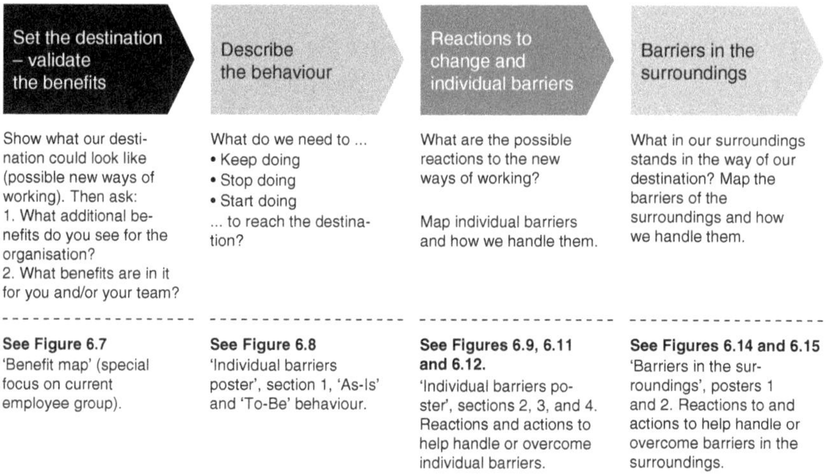

Set the destination – validate the benefits	Describe the behaviour	Reactions to change and individual barriers	Barriers in the surroundings
Show what our destination could look like (possible new ways of working). Then ask: 1. What additional benefits do you see for the organisation? 2. What benefits are in it for you and/or your team?	What do we need to ... • Keep doing • Stop doing • Start doing ... to reach the destination?	What are the possible reactions to the new ways of working? Map individual barriers and how we handle them.	What in our surroundings stands in the way of our destination? Map the barriers of the surroundings and how we handle them.
See Figure 6.7 'Benefit map' (special focus on current employee group).	**See Figure 6.8** 'Individual barriers poster', section 1, 'As-Is' and 'To-Be' behaviour.	**See Figures 6.9, 6.11 and 6.12.** 'Individual barriers poster', sections 2, 3, and 4. Reactions and actions to help handle or overcome individual barriers.	**See Figures 6.14 and 6.15** 'Barriers in the surroundings', posters 1 and 2. Reactions to and actions to help handle or overcome barriers in the surroundings.

Source: Designed by Mads Herskind, Helena Bograd, and Rasmus Rytter.

In 2017, the Maersk Tower was officially inaugurated as an extension of the University of Copenhagen's Faculty of Health and Medical Sciences facilities. The purpose of the tower is to further enable the faculty to become an important centre for world-class health research and education. In addition to research and teaching facilities, it also includes a sterilisation centre. Initially, the sterilisation centre handled the sterilisation of test tubes and other glass containers from a handful of departments at the Faculty of Health and Medical Sciences. However, the centre had the potential to handle all of the sterilisation of glass containers at the faculty and thus reduce the number of sterilisation centres from six to one. The sterilisation centre project was initiated to explore optimising the sterilisation task, identify whether high-quality glass sterilisation could be guaranteed for all faculty departments, ensure better safety, and create a better working environment for employees. The project had two purposes: an optimisation purpose (cost purpose) and a stakeholder satisfaction purpose.

The optimisation purpose was translated into a number of specific efficiency benefits, all driven by gathering the sterilisation process in one centre. The purposes related to quality, safety, and work environment came through improvements related to the standardisation of the sterilisation process and logistics. During the benefits realisation workshop, five employee groups were identified as needing to change behaviour to realise the benefits. The final benefit map is shown in Figure 6.7.

After the benefits realisation workshop, a change analysis was conducted to understand and estimate the change efforts required to realise the benefits. The change analysis included change workshops for the groups of employees who were facing the most significant changes.

The change workshop requires that we are able to present a picture of how the future ways of working could look like for each employee group after the change. It means that we often need to do some work in the technical track before conducting the workshop.

In the sterilisation centre project, one of the groups affected by the change comprised the lab managers and laboratory technicians, who were the primary users of glass containers for research purposes. We will use them as an example when we go through how to facilitate the change workshop.

Set the Destination: Validate the Benefits

The first part of the change workshop focuses on creating ownership of the change, benefits, and project. We are continually learning more about the project, so there has to be an openness to new inputs to benefits as long as they are within its boundaries.

Figure 6.7 The benefit map for the sterilisation centre project.

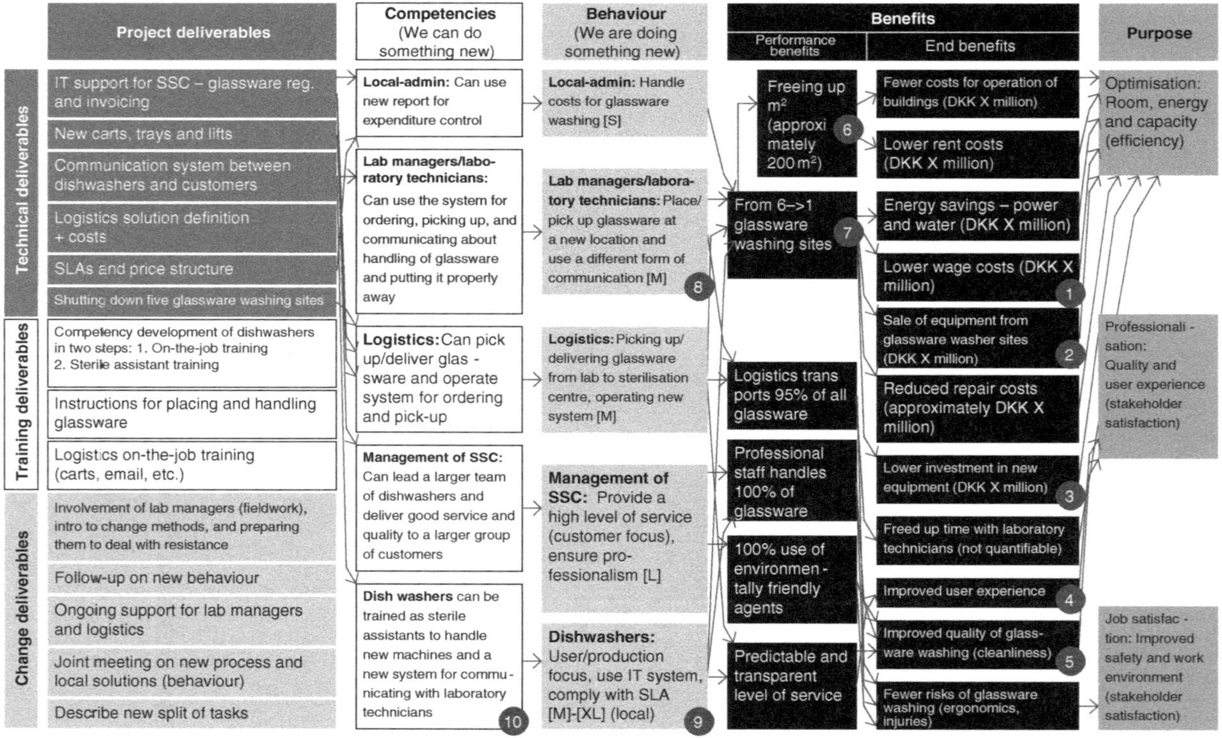

Project deliverables

Technical deliverables
IT support for SSC – glassware reg. and invoicing
New carts, trays and lifts
Communication system between dishwashers and customers
Logistics solution definition + costs
SLAs and price structure
Shutting down five glassware washing sites

Training deliverables
Competency development of dishwashers in two steps: 1. On-the-job training 2. Sterile assistant training
Instructions for placing and handling glassware
Logistics on-the-job training (carts, email, etc.)

Change deliverables
Involvement of lab managers (fieldwork), intro to change methods, and preparing them to deal with resistance
Follow-up on new behaviour
Ongoing support for lab managers and logistics
Joint meeting on new process and local solutions (behaviour)
Describe new split of tasks

Competencies (We can do something new)
Local-admin: Can use new report for expenditure control
Lab managers/laboratory technicians: Can use the system for ordering, picking up, and communicating about handling of glassware and putting it properly away
Logistics: Can pick up/deliver glassware and operate system for ordering and pick-up
Management of SSC: Can lead a larger team of dishwashers and deliver good service and quality to a larger group of customers
Dish washers can be trained as sterile assistants to handle new machines and a new system for communicating with laboratory technicians (10)

Behaviour (We are doing something new)
Local-admin: Handle costs for glassware washing [S]
Lab managers/laboratory technicians: Place/pick up glassware at a new location and use a different form of communication [M] (8)
Logistics: Picking up/delivering glassware from lab to sterilisation centre, operating new system [M]
Management of SSC: Provide a high level of service (customer focus), ensure professionalism [L]
Dishwashers: User/production focus, use IT system, comply with SLA [M]-[XL] (local) (9)

Benefits

Performance benefits
Freeing up m² (approximately 200 m²) (6)
From 6–>1 glassware washing sites (7)
Logistics transports 95% of all glassware
Professional staff handles 100% of glassware
100% use of environmentally friendly agents
Predictable and transparent level of service

End benefits
Fewer costs for operation of buildings (DKK X million)
Lower rent costs (DKK X million)
Energy savings – power and water (DKK X million)
Lower wage costs (DKK X million) (1)
Sale of equipment from glassware washer sites (DKK X million) (2)
Reduced repair costs (approximately DKK X million)
Lower investment in new equipment (DKK X million) (3)
Freed up time with laboratory technicians (not quantifiable)
Improved user experience (4)
Improved quality of glassware washing (cleanliness) (5)
Fewer risks of glassware washing (ergonomics, injuries)

Purpose
Optimisation: Room, energy and capacity (efficiency)
Professionalisation: Quality and user experience (stakeholder satisfaction)
Job satisfaction: Improved safety and work environment (stakeholder satisfaction)

The size of the change in the behaviour column is indicated for each group of employees in T-shirt sizes, varying from size S to XL. The numbers indicate the KPIs in the benefits realisation plan.

To introduce the project, we start by looking at the benefit map, which is still a rough draft after the benefits realisation workshop. Next, the participants are presented with the first ideas about the future ways of working. If the benefits we want depend on an optimised process, we could bring a draft of what the new process steps could look like and what tools or IT systems we assume would support it. The level of detail needed in the presentation of the future ways of working depends on the employee ambassadors and their managers and how used to designing their own future ways of working they are. If the people in the workshop are not usually involved in that type of work, we need to present a more detailed picture of their possible future ways of working.

When we have presented the purpose, benefits, and a sketch for the future ways of working, we ask the participants two questions:

- What additional benefits do you see for the organisation?
- What benefits are in it for you and/or your team?

The latter is by far the more important one. In most cases, many new benefits for the employees surface that the people working in the project never thought about. It could be things like, 'This will reduce the number of clicks considerably and thus reduce many of our colleagues' problems with golfer elbows stemming from using the mouse too much' or 'This will make it easier to coordinate with department X' or 'This will remove all of the frustration of misreading other colleagues' handwritten notes.' These benefits are usually not something that will impact the business case considerably, but they are extremely useful when building the case for change for that group of employees. Identifying these microbenefits also helps build a positive atmosphere for the rest of the workshop.[2]

[2] The script for the change workshop can be found in Box 6.6.

In the sterilisation centre project, lab managers and laboratory technicians were a vital part of the change. Therefore, it was essential to have them participate in a change workshop. The participants were the benefit owner and two lab managers who had not previously been involved in the project but only received a brief introduction. The introduction to the project and the discussion and validation of the benefits were based on an early version of the benefit map for the sterilisation centre (an early version of Figure 6.7) and a handheld demo of the new ways of working. As a result, we detailed and clarified a number of nonfinancial benefits for the business case and microbenefits for the lab managers. We were also able to refute some of the project manager's and benefit owners' concerns about how the change initiative would be received. It provided the foundation for further conversation about the new behaviour for lab managers and laboratory technicians.

Describe the Behaviour

The next step is to describe the behaviour we expect employees to have attained when the project is completed. Describing the new behaviour for a group of employees is threefold:

1. Describe the new behaviour for the groups of employees in question.
2. Describe and understand the current behaviour, including:
   - Specifying which behaviours should stop and which to continue doing;
   - Understanding the background of the current behaviour, especially if something seems counterintuitive.
3. Select a method for measuring and tracking the new behaviour.

In practice, the order of the first two steps to describe new behaviours may vary. It is often easier to talk about the new behaviour first, but if that is difficult, start with the current behaviour. When we talk about the new and current behaviour for a group of employees, in practice, it means the new or current behaviour for the task(s) we are working on which are changing. If the employees solve other tasks that are not affected by the change, they are not discussed.

Before completing the change analysis, the behaviour must be clearly described. In that way, we can determine whether an employee has attained the desired behaviour. There are often changes to our description of behaviour when we start to involve more people later on in the project. But if we do not make it concrete, it often becomes difficult to discuss the initial proposal for new behaviours with the rest of the employee group. Box 6.2 outlines the behavioural design principle.

Box 6.2: Behavioural design principle: make it easy

1. **Make it easy to do the right thing.** If it takes too much effort to change your ways of working, it is often the reason why our colleagues never start. If we can reduce the efforts required to embrace the new ways of working, getting our colleagues to change their behaviour becomes easier.
2. **Make new behaviour the standard.** When making one particular behaviour the standard way of working, our colleagues are more likely to choose that behaviour.
3. **Be specific: describe the visible behaviour.** What behaviour do we want to see? When describing behaviour, we must always focus on what we *see* ourselves or others do. Use words such as 'walk', 'click', and 'invite' and avoid words such as 'think', 'feel', 'experience', and 'understand'. By making it very clear what actions need to be taken, we increase the chance of it happening.

The current behaviour is divided into the behaviour we want to continue and the one we want to stop. It can be challenging to agree on what exactly the current behaviour entails. Therefore, we can settle for an imperfect picture of the tasks we need to continue doing, but we need to be very clear on the tasks we need to stop doing. The behaviour we want to stop doing is the key to freeing up time for new tasks or reducing cost.

Understand the Current Behaviour

If parts of the current behaviour look strange to outsiders, it is crucial to understand *why* that behaviour is carried out. Usually, behaviour is not primarily a result of employees' own thoughts and needs. It is mainly driven by the demands, inputs, and possibilities provided by the surroundings. Maybe there is a good explanation – or perhaps no one can remember why the workflow is as it is. Either way, this knowledge can be used to change behaviour or add important details to future behaviour (or perhaps continue doing the behaviour if there are good reasons for doing so).

The facilitation of the remainder of the change workshop can, in the same way as facilitating the development of the purpose, be carried out by going through a series of facilitation questions on posters. Figure 6.8 shows the current and new behaviours of lab managers and laboratory technicians from the sterilisation centre project.

The poster contains a number of basic information. 'Department/area/employee group' and 'Size' refer to the employee group from our benefit map. The T-shirt size refers to the size of the change we believe the employee group will face at the benefits realisation workshop. Additionally, we have added the name of the benefit owner and the project manager. The current and future behaviour is summarised in bullet points. The box in the bottom left describes the current behaviour.

Figure 6.8 'Individual barriers' poster', section 1: description of the new and current behaviours of lab managers and laboratory technicians.

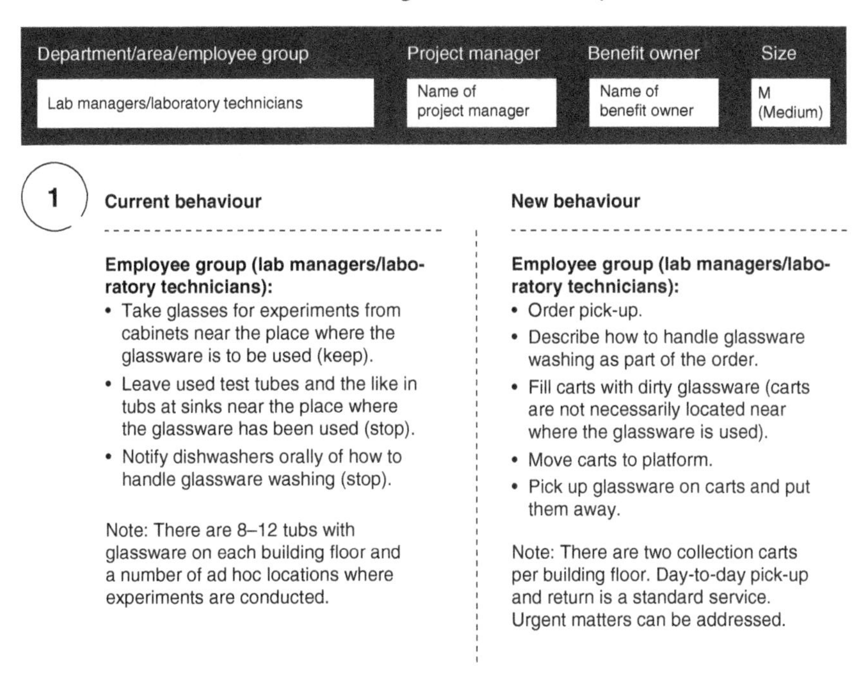

'Keep' means we continue doing it, and 'stop' means we should stop doing it. The box in the bottom right describes the new behaviour.

Measuring the New Behaviour

Once we have described the behaviour, we must define how we expect to track and measure the behaviour. That discussion requires that we are fairly precise in describing our expectations for the new behaviour. There are four methods to measure new behaviour:

- Behavioural data provided by IT systems.
- Questionnaire: ask about behaviour.

- Interviews.
- Observations.

The discussion on how to measure new behaviour must take place during the analysis phase as it has an impact on the cost of the project. Perhaps more technical deliverables will have to be produced if we want data on behaviour that does not exist today. Alternatively, we may need to invest a few hours in collecting questionnaire data or observing the new behaviour. The method we choose to measure the new behaviour will then be used as part of the activities when implementing the change in the execution phase. Box 6.3 depicts how it was part of the change efforts in the sterilisation centre project.

Box 6.3: Describe the new behaviour by using user stories

As an alternative to describing the new behaviour on a poster, as shown in Figure 6.8, consider whether you can use the format you are using to collect or document technical requirements. It can make it easier for project participants to describe the new behaviour and easier for both the project manager and project participants to jump from one project track to another since the tools are the same.

Example

Within the course of an agile transformation in an insurance company, user stories were introduced as a format for documenting user needs and developing requirements for agile software development. The agile transformation introduced a significant change for many employee groups, and

(Continued)

(Continued)

there was a need to describe what the new agile behaviour consisted of. Since user stories were already used to describe the user experience and thus understand the technical requirements, the insurance company chose the same method to describe the new, agile behaviour. A user story's title acts as a summary of the story's content, and the description of it is done like this:

'As a < role/person> I want to <requirement> so that <purpose>.'

In addition, acceptance criteria were defined to test whether or not the user story was implemented.

The agile transformation introduced a number of fixed meetings, the stand-up meeting being one of them. The purpose was to ensure that project participants identified and removed any impediment to development in a short period of time. Participants are standing during the meetings to help keep it short. Each participant was expected to answer three questions. The concept can be challenging to implement as stand-up meetings often require a change in the daily routine and a new way of approaching and discussing tasks.

Our user story for future behaviour at stand-up meetings looked like this:

Title: Daily stand-up meeting
Description: 'As a project manager, I want to facilitate daily stand-up meetings so that team members can coordinate with each other and identify possible impediments to development.'

(Continued)

(Continued)

To test whether or not our user story was being executed correctly, a number of acceptance criteria were established.

Acceptance criteria

- The team uses the structure: What did I do yesterday? What will I do today? Are there any impediments in my way, or do I have extra time to support others?
- Impediments (if any) are raised but not solved at the meeting.
- Each team member spends no more than one minute answering the questions.

The number of acceptance criteria reflected the extent of a user story. To understand the size of the change, we also created a user story for the current behaviour to identify what behaviour should continue and what behaviour should stop. With user stories for future and current behaviour, including an outline of acceptance criteria for future behaviour, in most cases, we could estimate the change efforts if we had reasonable knowledge of the colleagues in question.

The change that lab managers and laboratory technicians have to adapt to is, in isolation, a lower service level where they have to do a slightly greater part of the task of having glass containers sterilised. The practical task of ordering sterilisation, describing how to handle the glass containers, moving the used glass containers to another location, and putting clean glass containers back in place is not hard to learn. However, motivation may be hard to come by if the benefits of a uniform quality of glass cleaning do not correspond to the lower level of service. This particular change for the lab managers and laboratory technicians illustrates quite well how determining the size of a change does not simply consist of explaining the overall purpose and helping the employees fulfil a new task. The size of the change also depends on whether or not the employees like the change. Simply put: what's in it for them?

Reactions to Change: Individual Barriers

When identifying the change effort activities that will result in the new behaviour, we are trying to predict possible reactions to change. This aids us in creating a change process with as little resistance as possible.

Identifying and managing resistance is part of the change process. John Maxwell (2013) formulated the 20–50–30 rule, which states that, on average, 20% of employees will support your efforts to initiate change, 50% will be undecided, and the remaining 30% will resist. While Maxwell's rule may be too pessimistic in many cases, it serves as a reminder that resistance *will* appear and that we need to focus on the vast majority that is likely to aid our efforts in driving change. If we help our colleagues through a change in an effective way, we may avoid resistance from the 50% that are on the fence. Perhaps we can even win someone over from the resistance group. If not, we must ensure that the people showing great resistance do not hinder their colleagues from going through the change.

To identify potential resistance, we try to predict our colleagues' possible reactions to the change. Although we start by looking at each employee group, it often makes sense to look at the individual employees, as they will probably react differently to the change. The individual's attitude and motivation for change can be grouped based on four reactions to change.

Reactions to change

0 – I like it (no resistance – positive about the change).

1 – I don't get it (logical, rational reaction).

2 – I don't like it (emotional reaction).

3 – I don't like you (reaction based on a lack of trust).

Source: Adapted from Maurer (2010).

The individual employee's resistance to the change must be handled differently depending on the type of reaction. Lack of understanding can often be remedied by providing more information about why we are initiating change. On the other hand, if the resistance is based on an emotional reaction or lack of trust, a push of more information will often only reinforce resistance. If we introduce changes that deprive an employee of their status, for example introducing a new IT system causing an employee to go from being an IT expert to a user in line with the rest of the team, it can naturally create a resistance to change.

A practical approach to identifying reactions to change can be an individual brainstorming session among the manager(s) and employees who know the employee group. Framing the question as 'How might *your colleagues* react to the change?' is important for the quality of answers we get from the employees in the workshops. It removes the focus from the workshop participants to the whole group of employees. Once possible reactions have been identified and everyone understands them, they are coupled to the four reactions to change. In that way, we get an overview of potential resistance and what type they represent.

Finally, since we are priming people with more negative than positive reactions to change, we ask what they think the distribution between the four types of reactions will be. It helps us to get a balanced view of the individual barriers to change we are facing.

Example from the Sterilisation Centre Case Study

The case study on the sterilisation centre is an excellent example of how the involvement of a few lab managers makes us wiser to the extent of the change. Their knowledge of the current behaviour and what reactions they expected from their colleagues were crucial to how we planned to help them. The input from the two lab managers confirmed that the new way of handling glass cleaning would be perceived as a reduction in service level, but only a small reduction, and that most would see it as a minor sacrifice for the greater good. Figure 6.9 shows that the reactions to change does not necessarily only come from the impact of

Figure 6.9 'Individual barriers' poster, section 2: expected reactions and coupling to reactions to the change.

Brainstorming on expected thoughts on the change (step 1) **and coupling to reactions to change** (step 2)

Expected reactions (number and reaction type in parentheses)

- Unfavourable that some of the dishwashers might need to switch jobs. **(2 – 'I don't like it'. Emotional reaction).**
- Tiresome having to put glassware away. **(2 – 'I don't like it'. Emotional reaction).**
- Better quality washing (0 – "I like it").
- Resistance to getting glassware washed in a new place: 'They do not provide proper washing.' **(3 – 'I don't like you'.** Reaction to lack of trust).
- Difference between floors (there is a difference between subgroups of lab managers)
  – Floor X will think 'Fine' **(0 – 'I like it').**
- A fear of steps towards efficiency will eventually lead to layoffs. **(3 – 'I don't like you'.** Reaction to lack of trust).

Note: Many people will think that it is unfavourable, but it is a minor thing. We do not expect much resistance from the majority.

change on the colleagues in our team. The effects on other groups of employees can also influence reactions.

In addition to giving us new and valuable knowledge of the reactions to the change we might expect, the involvement of the two lab managers also helped to get them engaged in the project and prepare them for the role as committed ambassadors in the change process. Without input from colleagues who know the people who will be affected by the change and know their culture, norms, and work routines, it is challenging to make good suggestions on what the change efforts should contain.

Managing Individual Barriers

Once we have identified the individual barriers, we must describe the change activities to help individual employees and managers overcome them and thus get through the change process in the execution phase. Some of the change activities can be characterised as further efforts to prepare for the new ways of working, while other change activities consist of supporting the anchoring of the new behaviour. In some projects, the transition between preparation and actual support to anchor new behaviour is marked by a technical launch. In other cases, the transition is more fluid.[3]

The first part of the preparation often consists of a field study, ensuring that we thoroughly understand each employee group's current situation and behaviours through analysis, data collection, and field research. The preparation also includes the employees' involvement in designing the future behaviour, for example by preparing a script for new behaviour[4] and building the competencies that are a prerequisite for the new behaviour. Involving employees is an essential part of the preparation, which

---

[3] Figure 8.1 shows the process of change during the execution phase, where the start of the broad organisational implementation is often marked by a technical launch.

[4] The development of a script for new behaviour is described in Box 8.2.

is also an activity that helps reduce resistance. We frontload the change efforts, often by involving people early in the process to reduce the overall change efforts needed to change behaviour. If we succeed in designing the new behaviour to become easy to practise, we can further reduce both the resistance to change and other efforts to implement the new ways of working.

The preparation part of the change activities will typically consist of these activities:

- Further development of the change story.
- Field studies 'on the floor', where we learn more about the actual behaviour and the reasons behind it.
- Clarification and adjustment of new behaviour in collaboration with employees, for example by developing a script for new behaviour.
- Mobilisation, competency development, and support of the first-line managers and employee ambassadors who will help make the change happen.
- General competency building, for example through training.
- Stakeholder analysis, communication plans, and updated execution plans and estimates.

The change activities related to changing behaviour are done primarily by first-line managers and ambassadors who help their colleagues overcome resistance. Targeted communication efforts must also support these activities.

How to Handle 'I Don't Get It' Reactions to Change

Change activities are often simplified to handle type 1 resistance reactions, i.e. resistance stemming from a lack of information and understanding. An effective means to handle this type of resistance is to tell the story about the purpose of the change and provide information on the 'how' at meetings, events, in writing, and via formal 1:1 conversations or conversations at the coffee machine. Storytelling helps us to understand the 'why' and creates a sense of meaning. Some of the resistance can arise due to confusion about the implications of the change. The larger and more complex a change is, the greater part of the communication will typically be given by first-line managers in small forums or 1:1. Ensuring that our colleagues understand the meaning of the change and avoiding confusion are essential and typically the easiest part of the change efforts.

It often takes more to help colleagues who have types 2 and 3 reactions to the change. Emotional reactions or reactions based on a lack of trust are often not clearly expressed. Although a colleague may express an 'I don't get it' reaction, it may very well mask a type 2 or 3 reaction. In the example of the IT expert, the employee may not express a type 2 reaction based on the fear of a loss of status, as it would be an expression of putting themselves above the organisation. It is probably more likely that the employee expresses a type 1 resistance or is just sitting on the fence. Thus, the work of clarifying the individual employee's reactions to change may turn out to be substantial.

Articulate the Fear

Storytelling can be an effective tool to increase positivity and enthusiasm about the aspects of the change affecting the group. The message of what each employee group gets out of the change effort is important, just as it is also important to address fear, such as the fear of not being able to do their job after the change or the fear of being fired. Later, in step 2 of the change workshop, I describe the need for competencies. If the employees do not have the competencies needed to fulfil their jobs in the future, it must be communicated how to handle that issue in a way that does not create fear.

Secondly, we must be honest about all implications of the change – also the less positive ones. If not, the employees lose their trust in us. Building trust is key to reducing type 3 reactions. Trust is also crucial to our ability to deal with resistance. In many cases, high levels of trust are also the reason some of our colleagues are positive towards the change, even if they do not know everything about it yet. Trust is a hard change currency. The need for trust in the relationship between project representatives and those who need to change their behaviour is the reason why first-line managers and key employees are the primary ones to represent the project. That is also why a large part of the project team's change efforts will consist of helping first-line managers and employee ambassadors to make change happen. This way of bringing about change is therefore often called 'backstage leadership'. Box 6.4 delves into the role of the ambassador.

Box 6.4: The ambassador must also be an activist

The employees we choose to involve early on should have the best foundation to help their colleagues through the change. They must fulfil the role of the classic superuser, have a strong internal network, and the trust of their colleagues. On top of this, they must be activists, proactively encouraging and helping their colleagues change their behaviour. Some may already have taken up that role, but many will need help. It can be a little scary to actively go out and proactively encourage your colleagues to make change happen, so the potential to be a good activist is an important criterion when selecting ambassadors.

Backstage Leadership in Practice

Backstage leadership may have a slightly sinister sound to it, but it has nothing to do with management or leadership of a shady character. Backstage leadership aims to make change happen by using the trust that already exists in informal groups and networks between first-line managers or ambassadors and the rest of the employees. See Figure 6.10 and Box 6.5.

Backstage leadership must ensure that our first-line managers and ambassadors can make change happen in their department, group, or network. It should give them the coaching, training, and tools they need to bring about change. Part of the effort happens during the analysis phase as part of our preparations before the new ways of working are introduced, and a lot happens as we help make the new behaviour stick. An important

Figure 6.10 Backstage leadership.

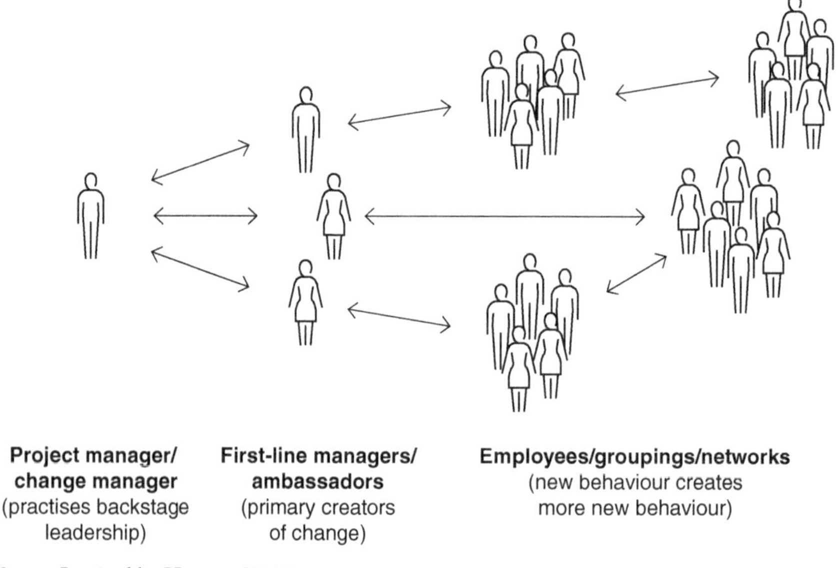

Source: Inspired by Herrero (2011).

element in maintaining and building trust in all links of the network is to be open about successes and challenges and share information between the person responsible for the change, first-line managers, ambassadors, and the employees who are going to change their behaviour. That network becomes an important source of knowledge about what works and what does not work as well as getting a feel for the attitude towards the change in each department or group.

It must be addressed if there are trust issues between people in the employee group and the first-line manager or the ambassadors they need to work with. It could also be between people in the project change track and the first-line managers or ambassadors. Building trust in a relationship can take a long time. Therefore, one solution may be to switch roles in the project or even remove people from the project or the ambassador role. If you choose to work on building trust in the relationship, Maister et al.'s (2002) trust equation can help you understand what variables you can work on to improve your trustworthiness. Hopefully, if you improve your trustworthiness, other people are more likely to place their trust in you.

Box 6.5: The trust equation

Change management is very much about benefitting from the trust that already exists in the organisation and building on that by ensuring that information is effectively shared in the network between employees, first-line managers, ambassadors, and project management. Therefore, we often talk about how trust in the network helps to create the foundation for benefits realisation. Trust as a formula can sound a

(Continued)

(Continued)

bit strange, but that is precisely what David Maister has done.[5] He has described the trust equation this way:

$$\text{Trustworthiness} = \frac{\text{Credibility} + \text{Reliability} + \text{Intimacy}}{\text{Self} - \text{orientation}}$$

The greater the trust in the network between the employees, first-line manager or an ambassador, and the backstage leader is, the greater the odds are of making the change happen. If you are a first-line manager, ambassador, or change manager doing backstage leadership, you will be measured in terms of trust. You will be judged on whether your colleagues can trust what you say (credibility), trust you to do what you say (reliability), and feel safe discussing other topics than project work (intimacy). Also, the care, interest, and attention you give to others or how occupied you are about how things affect you (self-orientation) is part of the assessment.

Thus, your trustworthiness equals the sum of credibility, reliability, and intimacy divided by your self-orientation.

Tools for Changing Behaviour

Although trust is not explicitly part of the change activities, the level of trust determines how effective our actions are in helping people who are not embracing the change. Activities aimed at anchoring new behaviour typically include the following:

- First-line managers' and ambassadors' coaching and influence on the members of the employee group.

[5] Maister et al. (2002).

- Support for first-line managers and ambassadors (backstage leadership).
- Simulation testing and redesign of new behaviour/new ways of working.
- Status meetings, pulse checks, or other ways to track progress.
- Storytelling (beyond the 1:1 situation).

In Part 3, I discuss, among others, field studies, workshops for developing scripts for new behaviours, simulation testing behaviours, and measuring progress for first-line managers and backstage leaders to use. In addition to the methods I go through in this book, several other tools can be used.[6] The choice of method should depend partly on the change in question, partly on the target group's knowledge of the tools, and partly on what you have the best experience with.

As Figure 6.11 shows, we defined a number of preparatory change activities and activities to implement the change in the sterilisation centre case. As a facilitator, it is often a good idea to include examples of change activities when you, the first-line manager, and ambassadors are going to identify the activities that can have the greatest impact. It provides the best opportunity to discuss how change can be helped along the way. After all, the first-line managers and ambassadors are probably good at what they do, but it is usually not change management, which is why a little inspiration often helps get a better result. Although the change for lab managers and laboratory technicians was not so extensive, we used a variety of change activities, just in a minimised format, to fit the size of the change. For example, the field study simply consisted of visiting each floor and observing how the tasks were solved and having a lab manager explain the background of the current behaviour.

[6]There are several change models and tools that can be used as a supplement or alternatives to the tools presented in the book. Among others, Prosci has a number of excellent tools and a model for individual change (ADKAR), which is often used as a supplement.

Figure 6.11 'Individual barriers' poster, section 3: change activities for lab managers and laboratory technicians (the sterilisation centre case).

Change activities

Preparatory change activities
- Completion of the story – adjustment to main arguments and dissemination.
- Understand the situation on each floor (field studies).
- Preparing first-line managers and ambassadors among the employees (the selected lab managers) for communicating the story and dealing with resistance.
- Design of behaviour together with lab managers and laboratory technicians (employees) on each floor.

Activities to implement the change
- Ongoing sparring with managers and ambassadors.
- Managers' and ambassadors' 1:1 sparring with employees.
- Assessing and adjusting the new behaviour to ensure that it works with new behaviour of dishwashers, logistics and introduction of upgraded tools.
- Status meetings where the adaption of new behaviour is measured (observation and data collection from sterilisation centre).

Just as the individual employee groups serve as the basis for defining the change effort activities, they are also used as the foundation for describing the training efforts and identifying the requirements for the technical deliverables.

Define the Need for New Competencies and How to Develop Them

The easiest part of making change happen is usually raising the level of competency. The first step is to identify what new competencies the group of employees need to acquire to be able to change their behaviour. The next step is to describe how to develop the new competencies. Here we start by looking at the results from the benefits realisation workshop. As with the rest of the change analysis, we need to take two or three steps further based on the more detailed knowledge we now have about the desired behaviour of the employee group. We do this by updating and clarifying the list of competencies from each group of employees that we made at the benefits realisation workshop. If there are significant differences in what competencies each employee needs within a group, you can divide them into several subgroups.

The choice of learning method, ensuring the building of competencies, varies depending on needs, the possibilities of bringing the group of employees together, etc. There are several different learning methods to choose from, such as traditional classroom training, e-learning, webinar, reading, or on-the-job training. Again, it is about finding the format or mix of formats that best suits the individual group of employees.

In principle, identifying change activities and describing the need for acquiring new competencies can be done in one step at the change workshop. But these two activities should be separated. Otherwise, we risk losing focus on the change activities as this is often the most difficult part because many participants will not have much experience participating in change activities. The result of our efforts in this part of the workshop can be summarised for each employee group on the 'Individual barriers' poster, as shown in Figure 6.12.

When we have finished detailing the new behaviour and have described change activities and activities to acquire new competencies, we are through three of the four steps in the change workshop. We are thus finished with the part of the barrier wheel in Figure 6.5 that relates to the individual. All that is left is to identify barriers to the new behaviour in the employees' surroundings and how to remove or reduce them.

Barriers in the Surroundings Identification and Handling

In the barrier analysis, when we go from looking at barriers in the individual space to also looking at barriers in the employees' surroundings, it is a way to see change management in a broader perspective. It provides an overview of all the other parameters that may influence behaviour and creates a need to work systematically with them, ensuring as much efficiency and success with our change efforts as possible.

Figure 6.12 'Individual barriers' poster: identification of new behaviour, change activities, and activities for acquiring competencies.

Department/area/employee group

Lab managers/laboratory technicians at Panum

Current behaviour

Employee group (lab managers/ laboratory technicians):

- Take glasses for experiments from cabinets near the place where the glassware is to be used **(keep)**.
- Leave used test tubes and the like in tubs at sinks near the place where the glassware has been used **(stop)**.
- Notify dishwashers orally of how to handle glassware washing **(stop)**.

Note: There are 8–12 tubs with glassware on each building floor and a number of ad hoc locations where experiments are conducted.

New behaviour

Employee group (lab managers/ laboratory technicians):

- Order pick-up.
- Describe how to handle glassware washing as part of the order.
- Fill carts with dirty glassware (carts are not necessarily located near where the glassware is used).
- Move carts to platform.
- Pick up glassware on carts and put them away.

Note: there are two collection carts per building floor. Day-to-day pick-up and return is a standard service. Urgent matters can be addressed.

Brainstorming on expected thoughts on the change (step 1) **and coupling to reactions to change** (step 2)

Expected reactions (resistance level in brackets)

- Unfavourable that some of the dishwashers might need to switch jobs **(2 – 'I don't like it.'** Emotional reaction).
- Tiresome having to put glassware away **(2 – 'I don't like it.'** Emotional reaction).
- Better quality washing **(0 – 'I like it')**.
- Resistance to getting glassware washed in a new place: 'They do not provide proper washing' **(3 – 'I don't like you.'** Reaction to lack of trust).
- Difference between floors (there is a difference between subgroups of lab managers) – Floor X will think 'Fine' **(0 – 'I like it')**.
- A fear of steps towards efficiency will eventually lead to layoffs **(0 – 'I don't like you.'** Reaction to lack of trust).

Note: many people will think that it is unfavourable, but it is a minor thing. We do not expect much resistance from the majority.

Project manager	Benefit owner	Size
Name of project manager	Name of benefit owner	M (Medium)

3 Change activities

Preparatory change activities

- Completion of the story – adjustment to main arguments and dissemination.
- Understand the situation on each floor (field studies).
- Prepare the first-line managers and ambassadors among the employees (the selected lab managers) for communicating the story and deal with resistance.
- Design of behaviour together with lab managers and laboratory technicians (employees) on each floor.

Activities to implement the change

- Ongoing sparring with managers and ambassadors.
- Managers' and ambassadors' 1:1 sparring with employees.
- Assessing and adjusting the new behaviour to ensure that it works with the new behaviour of dish-washers, logistics, and the introduction of upgraded tools.
- Status meetings where the adaption of new behaviour is measured (observation and data collection from sterilisation centre).

4 The employee group's need for and how to build new competencies

1. Define the competency requirements of the employee group (lab manager)

- Must be able to operate 'system' for ordering pick-up and description of handling of dishwashing.
- Must know where clean glassware should be placed and where it is picked up as well as how to operate carts.

2. Method for competency building (form of learning)

- Training in 'system', where carts should be placed and how carts are operated.
- Possibility of asking ambassadors questions.

Figure 6.13 Organisational and technical barriers (depicting parts of Figure 6.5).

Organisational barriers	Technical barriers
Groups	**Technology and physical environment**
Is there anything in the group that works against new behaviour? For example, in language or conversations or in the attitude towards management? Are there groups in the group?	Are the technological tools adequate and intuitive? Do they support or obstruct the desired behaviour? How do the office decor, lighting, etc., back up the current behaviour, and does it work for the new behaviour?
Organisational structure	**Processes**
Are there any factors in the organisation that counteract the desired behaviour? For example, in rules, values, incentives, resources, or organisational structure?	In what way is the current process related to behaviour? Do we need to change processes or procedures? What habits are currently an integrated part of our work life, and should we change them?
Culture and norms	**Products and services**
Do the organisational culture and norms enable the desired behaviour, or are there organisational culture and norms that stand in the way of our being able to create change?	What new products or services, if any, are necessary to implement the new behaviour?

Source: Designed by Mads Herskind and Rasmus Rytter.

Barriers unrelated to the individual can be divided into two groups: organisational barriers and technical barriers. Organisational barriers involve dealing with challenges at group and organisational levels, including the norms and culture in the organisation, which can inhibit change. Technical barriers address the technical enablers that need to be in place to succeed. Figure 6.13 shows both organisational and technical barriers. These barriers either require or affect the individual's ability to change behaviour and determine whether it will be easy or not. Both groups can be divided into three types of barriers, leaving us with a checklist of six barrier types. The individual employee groups may experience all, only a few, or none of the six barrier types.

The Sterilisation Centre as an Example

The case study on the sterilisation centre's lab managers and laboratory technicians was not typical, because we identified all six types of barriers for the employee group. If we look at the organisational barriers, lab managers and laboratory technicians consist of many subgroups, each accustomed to their own level of service (group barrier). They have different ideas about whether one joint sterilisation centre can provide them with the same quality and service that they are currently getting from their local sterilisation centre. Establishing a new organisation with one central sterilisation centre and logistics service to handle glass transport is crucial to the shift from six sterilisation centres to one (organisational structure barrier). At the same time, the university has a clear focus on creating the best environment for researchers, where ideas about centralisation or standardisation are often received with some scepticism (norm and cultural barriers). The project must address these potential barriers carefully and avoid overestimating their impact.

The technical barriers were initially about figuring out how lab managers and laboratory technicians should communicate with the sterilisation centre, find solutions for how to store clean and dirty glass containers, and how to transport glass containers to and from the sterilisation centre, probably using small transport carts (technology, physical, and process barriers). The communication system was initially intended as an IT solution. Lab managers and laboratory technicians would use handheld scanners and iPads to register and communicate with logistics and cleaning personnel about the time of collection and return and what types of cleaning (products and service barrier) were needed. However, the acquisition of such a system would take a long time. At the change workshop, we therefore discussed a number of more simple solutions.

How Easily Can It Be Done?

One of the lab managers suggested we start with a piece of laminated paper on which lab managers and laboratory technicians could tick off what type of cleaning they needed and add a short comment if relevant. Communication about collection and return could then be done by email via a joint mailbox, which both logistics and cleaning personnel had access to. The solution was a technical minimum viable product[7] that could be used immediately and provide valuable learning about the exact need (if any) for a more advanced IT solution. No matter how advanced the technological solution was, new processes or workflows had to be created to order and buy new glass containers. The level of service also had to be formalised, and finally, it had to be decided what types of glass containers were allowed. The use of glass containers and the current level of service varied somewhat and were, therefore, two parameters that would significantly impact how the project would be accepted. Facilitating the task of identifying the technical and organisational barriers at the change workshop also took place with the help of a poster, which you can see in Figure 6.14.

The Interaction Between the Tracks

While the mapping and handling of the organisational barriers occur in the change track, the mapping of the technical barriers is a direct input to the technical track and the development of new IT, new processes, products, or services. The need for integration between the technical track and change tracks is great. The technical track provides input to make a demo of a possible

[7]The minimum viable product (abbreviated MVP) is defined by Ries (2017) as that version of a new product which allows a team to collect the maximum amount of validated learning about customers with the least effort, i.e. learning based on data instead of assumptions. MVP is also used to describe the smallest possible product or service to launch and create value for customers, citizens, or users.

Figure 6.14 'Barriers in the surroundings', poster 1: identification of organisational and technical barriers.

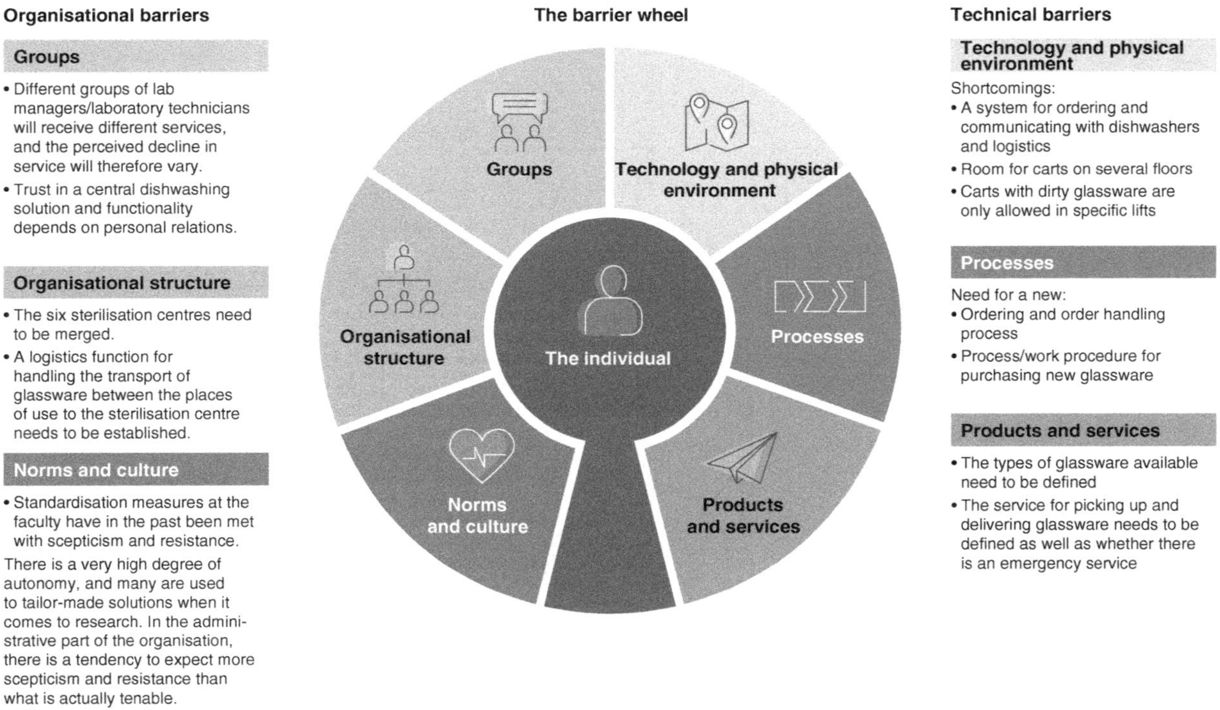

Source: Designed by Mads Herskind and Rasmus Rytter with inspiration from Grech et al. (2008).

future at the beginning of the change workshop. At the change workshop, we take the next step and identify high-level requirements for the technical track, and so the exchange of ideas and refinement of requirements should continue throughout the project. In some cases, parts of the technical deliverables may already be defined due to financial and technical limitations. In that case, the requirements from the change track serve as validation of the technical deliverables so we do not end up doing something we cannot use or do not need.

Just as the output from this part of the change workshop is often high-level requirements for handling technical barriers, the same may apply to the organisational and individual barriers we identified earlier. The output is often the basis for further analysis rather than the final result.

Identify New Change Activities and Specify Requirements for the Technical Track

Once we have identified the organisational and technical barriers to change, the next step is to identify specific solutions or requirements to ensure that we can overcome the barriers. For each group of employees where barriers are identified, we describe a solution and assign a priority and an owner. The owner of the organisational barriers will often be the benefit owner, as the owner must be mandated to ensure that the solution is implemented, possibly aided by the project. If the barrier is technical in nature, it will be solved in the technical track. The owner defines the solution to individual and organisational barriers in collaboration with the project manager, change manager, and remaining workshop participants.

Each solution is given a priority based on importance, for example 'High', 'Medium', or 'Low'. If the priority is high, implementing the solution is crucial to executing the change successfully. Figure 6.15 illustrates how the barriers we identified in the case study on the sterilisation centre are handled, prioritised, and assigned to an owner.

The quality criterion for the solutions is that they can all be estimated with the same certainty that we estimate the technical deliverables at the end of the analysis phase. Most of the time, this cannot be done at the workshop, so there is usually analysis work to be done afterwards.

Figure 6.15 'Barriers in the surroundings', poster 2: handling of organisational and technical barriers.

	Barriers	Handling/requirements	Priority	Owner
Organisational barriers				
Groups	• Different groups of lab managers/laboratory technicians receive different levels of service. • Trust in the quality from the new sterilisation centre is person dependent.	• The different groups of lab managers/laboratory technicians should be handled differently. • Special focus on employees who are concerned about quality. • Use the most positive groups as a good example or pilot.	• High • High • N/A	Project: (PM name) Steerco: (Benefit owner's name)
Organisation	• The six sterilisation centres need to be merged. • A logistics function for handling the transport of glassware between the places of use to the sterilisation centre needs to be established.	• Close five sterilisation centres. • Prepare the largest sterilisation centre for handling dishes from the entire faculty. • Build logistics function.	• High (not MVP) • High (not MVP) • High	Project: (PM name) Steerco: (Primary benefit owner's name)
Norms and culture	• Standardisation measures at the faculty have in the past been met with scepticism and resistance.	• High involvement of each of the individual employee groups in relation to the size of the change. • Invest in making it as easy as possible for lab managers/laboratory technicians.	• High • Medium	Project: (PM name) Steerco: (Primary benefit owner's name)

(*Continued*)

	Barriers	Handling/requirements	Priority	Owner
Organisational barriers				
Technology and physical environment	• A system for ordering and communicating with dishwashers. • Lack of room for carts on several floors. • Carts with dirty glassware are only allowed in specific lifts.	• A system for ordering and communicating with dishwashers is to be made. The MVP can be a marker and a laminated piece of paper. • Create space for the carts on each floor. • Any security problem must be examined, and agreements on the use of lifts must be in place.	• High (IT sys. not MVP) • Medium • High	Project: "PM name" Steerco: "Primary benefit owner's name"
Processes	• Ordering and order handling process are not in place. • Process/work procedure for purchasing new glassware.	• A process/work procedure for ordering and order handling must be made. • Process/work procedure for purchasing new glassware must be made.	• High • Medium (not MVP)	Project: "PM name" Steerco: "Primary benefit owner's name"
Products and services	• The types of glassware available need to be defined. • The service for picking up and delivering glassware needs to be defined and whether there is an emergency service.	• Involvement of individual employee groups to determine selection. • Involvement of each of the groups to determine needs.	• High (not MVP) • High (not MVP)	Project: "PM name" Steerco: "Benefit owner's name"

Source: Designed by Mads Herskind and Rasmus Rytter.
Steerco: steering committee.

Estimate and Plan the Change

Once we have conducted change workshops for the most critical employee groups, we have gained a good idea about what it takes to make the change happen. The next important step is to analyse, clarify, estimate, and plan the change activities.

Planning the change process often requires additional involvement of first-line managers and employees or others who can help gain the necessary knowledge. The result of the task of clarifying and estimating the change activities for each group of employees typically ends with the estimates being divided into four parts:

- Employee cost (employees who will be affected by the change – measured in hours or money either by using an hourly rate or by assessing the productivity loss).
- First-line managers' and ambassadors' cost.
- Support cost for managers and ambassadors.
- Cost for training/developing new competencies.

Employee cost includes the cost of time that passes until the employee group exhibits the desired behaviour. It can be time spent in meetings, seeking and receiving help, and becoming effective again after the change process. It is time that could have been spent on other work activities and therefore represents a loss of productivity. The estimates on employee time are almost always subject to a high amount of uncertainty. Still, the sum of time lost from operational work must be included, as this can be a considerable cost element in the business case and thus also a significant motivation to invest in making change happen quickly.

First-line managers' and ambassadors' cost is derived from the time they need to implement the change among the employee group or network they are in charge (or part) of. First-line managers and ambassadors must participate in most preparatory change activities to understand and establish ownership of the change. After that, time is spent helping employees and colleagues through resistance or giving them the competencies and support needed to get the new ways of working fully in place. Finally, they will participate in project meetings and receive coaching on how best to solve the challenges.

Support for first-line managers and ambassadors comes either from the project manager or a change manager responsible for the change track. It includes identifying and mobilising managers and ambassadors who are not already involved, planning and facilitating preparatory change activities that enable first-line managers and ambassadors to bring about change locally.

Estimating Time Consumption

It can be challenging to estimate the time the employees, first-line managers, and ambassadors will spend and how much support they need to make change happen in an employee group. It will vary with the size of the change, the size of the group, as well as:

- First-line managers' and ambassadors' experience in helping bring about change.
- The position of first-line managers and ambassadors in the employee group or network.
- The project manager's or change manager's expertise in supporting first-line managers and ambassadors.

If the estimates have a high level of uncertainty, then do what you would have done if you were estimating the design and development of an IT system or a process. Break down the task into smaller parts and draw on your colleagues' experience. Suppose the organisation does not have much experience in estimating the cost of change efforts. In that case, breaking down the change efforts does not always reduce uncertainty as much as we would like. It does, however, provide transparency about the prerequisites for the change efforts and knowledge about where the organisation needs to improve to get better at estimating the change efforts.

The part of the competency effort that does not happen as a result of on-the-job training is often done through more formal classroom training. Training is a well-known task in most organisations, and it includes time spent on material development, conducting the training itself, testing, and following up. In order to get the overall estimate of the change, the estimates for the individual employee groups are added together. Further, the change activities that cut across employee groups, such as developing the story and keeping track of change progress, are also included in the estimates for conducting the change track.

Splitting Tasks Between Tracks

The estimation of the technical deliverables takes place in the technical track, and the estimation of the organisational barriers takes place in the change track. If the content of the technical track is a piece of laminated paper and a new mailbox, the sharp division is less important. However, as a general rule, the tasks should be estimated by the people who are in the best position to do so.

The estimates for overcoming organisational barriers, such as the estimates for changing behaviour for the employee groups, can be difficult because experience is often sparse.

The estimation techniques used to estimate the change efforts are no different from those used to break down and estimate the technical deliverables.[8] Relative estimation, such as using T-shirt sizes, three-point estimation, or other classic estimation methods, can be used for both organisational and technical barriers. If your experience in estimating change efforts is limited, choose one method and do the best you can. It is important to start getting estimates for the change efforts, even if our first estimates are not that good. When you get more experienced, the aim should be to get estimates of the change efforts that are just as reliable as the estimates for the technical deliverables.

You have almost finished Part 2 and should now be ready to do the work to succeed with both the benefit track and the change track in the analysis phase. We have gone through the benefit-driven project design to establish the purpose and then take the next step at the benefits realisation workshop, where we established an overview of the entire project and how it creates value.

---

[8] See, for example, Olsson et al. (2019).

We have detailed how the benefits are estimated and made specific enough to enable us to track the benefits using the benefits realisation plan. We have been through the change workshop and what it takes to get the same overview of activities and deliverables as well as comparable quality of estimates in the change track that we have in the technical track. We are now ready for the steering committee and portfolio management to decide whether the project is attractive enough to continue. If the project is approved, you now have a solid basis for success. The analysis has already created ownership of the project among the benefit owner, first-line managers, and employee ambassadors – and by focusing on all three tracks in the project, you have made the best possible foundation for the project. The execution phase, which I will go through in Part 3, is now pending.

Box 6.6 contains a detailed script for the change workshop.

Box 6.6: The change workshop: a practical guide

The change workshop initiates the work in the change track in the analysis phase, and it is the first element in our structured approach to working with change management.

Desired workshop result

- Create ownership of the project's benefits and the upcoming change process.
- Identify 'what benefits are in it for them'.
- Define the necessary new behaviours and competencies as well as requirements for the technical deliverables derived by the need to enable new behaviour.

(*Continued*)

(*Continued*)

- Deliver the first version of the list of activities the change track needs to deliver to develop new behaviours and competencies.
- Prepare estimates and plans for the change track or prepare a plan for how estimates and plans for the change track are established as part of the analysis phase.

Before the workshop

Before the workshop, there are several tasks to be addressed:

- Conduct the benefits realisation workshop to design the project and ensure ownership of the benefits and the change among the benefit owners.
- Prepare a simple demo of the possible new ways of working.
- Mobilise first-line managers and future employee ambassadors.
- Prepare facilitation.

The most challenging facilitation task is to define specific change activities. In order to ensure ownership, the first-line managers and ambassadors themselves must participate in selecting change activities. As a facilitator, you should think about what change activities might be relevant. Consider bringing a catalogue of relevant change activities to draw inspiration from.

(*Continued*)

(*Continued*)

During the workshop

The standard agenda for the change workshop looks like this:

- Welcome, workshop purpose, agenda, and a brief introduction to the project (10 minutes).
- A brief introduction to the project's benefit map and elaboration of key points from the benefits realisation workshop (10 minutes).
- Demo of the possible new ways of working (20 minutes).
- Workshop, parts 1 to 5 (3.5 to 4.5 hours + lunch).
- Recap and next step (15 minutes).

Elaboration of workshop parts 1 to 5

The workshop is rolled out step by step, with recaps along the way. It is possible to facilitate the work on three employee groups at the same time. In these cases, joint recaps can be made to share inspiration and experience.

Part 1: Set the destination: validate the project benefits and identify 'What benefits are in it for us?' (approx. 30 minutes)

Ask the two questions below, and let the participants reflect on their answers in groups of two or three.

Reflection questions:

- What additional benefits do you see for the organisation?
- What benefits are in it for you and/or your team?

(*Continued*)

(*Continued*)

Recap of part 1: spend most of the time following up on the second question, as this is important input for the change effort, and it helps build a positive atmosphere for the remainder of the workshop.

Part 2: Describe the behaviour (approx. 30–45 minutes)

Use 'Individual barriers' poster, section 1 (Figure 6.8). It will take longer if you work with two or three employee groups in parallel.

- Define the new behaviour you want from the employee group.
- Sketch the current behaviour, primarily focusing on what you want employees to stop doing.
- Recap/presentation.

Part 3: Reactions to change and individual barriers (approx. 60–90 minutes)

Use sections 2, 3, and 4 of Figure 6.12. It will take longer if you work with two or three employee groups in parallel.

- Introduce/recap the four reactions to change (0: I like it, 1: I don't get it, 2: I don't like it, 3: I don't like you).
- Brainstorm (start with an individual brainstorm) on the reactions to change ('Individual barriers' poster, section 2).
- Frame the question as: 'How might *your colleagues* react to the change?' to get the best answers. This way of

(*Continued*)

(Continued)

asking puts focus on the whole group of employees and not just the employee ambassadors participating in the workshop.

- Use the four types of reactions to change to categorise the brainstorming output.
- Ask the participants about the likely distribution of reactions, for example in percentages for each of the four reactions to change.
- Recap/presentation.
- Provide an overview of possible change activities as inspiration for the next step.
- Define the deliverables and activities needed to create the desired behaviour ('Individual barriers' poster, section 3).
- Define the competencies that each employee group needs to develop and the activities needed to acquire the desired competencies ('Individual barriers' poster, section 4).
- Recap/presentation.

Part 4: Barriers in the surroundings (approx. 60–90 minutes)

Use 'Barriers in the surroundings', posters 1 and 2. It will take longer if you work with two or three employee groups in parallel.

- Identify the current barriers ('Barriers in the surroundings', poster 1).
- Recap/presentation.

(Continued)

(Continued)

- Define specific deliverables, activities or requirements for dealing with the identified barriers ('Barriers in the surroundings', poster 2).
- Recap/presentation.

Part 5: Estimate and plan (approx. 30–60 minutes)

In small-scale projects, estimate and plan the change.

- Estimate change deliverables and their underlying activities.
- Make the first draft of the plan for making change happen (the final plan is synchronised with the plan for the technical track).

In other projects, plan the rest of the analysis phase for the change track to clarify the activities needed to analyse, plan, and estimate the change efforts in the execution phase.

After the workshop

The work the change track must be continually coordinated with the results and knowledge accumulated in the benefit track and technical track during the analysis phase until the output and results from the three project tracks are presented together at the end of this phase.

Tip: timebox the individual elements of the workshop. If you run out of time, part 5 is usually the easiest part to postpone.

(Continued)

(*Continued*)

Format	Workshop
Materials	Posters for steps 2–4 of the workshop Prepare reflection questions for part 1 and use the planning tool you usually use for collaborative planning for part 5
Duration	5 hours if working with one employee group 6 hours if working with two or three employee groups in parallel
Participants	First-line managers and ambassadors, the project manager and/or change manager, and, if needed, a change specialist to aid in the facilitation
Result	Clarity of what benefits are in it for each employee group, the first draft of the description of new behaviour per employee group, what reactions to expect from each employee group, change activities, and initial estimates and plans

Part III

Lead the Change and Maximise Benefits Realisation

7

Maximising Benefits Realisation

Once the steering committee and portfolio board have evaluated and prioritised the project to continue to the execution phase, the real work begins to embed the change and the technical deliverables needed to realise the desired benefits.

Completing the work in the analysis phase of the benefit track, change track, and technical track is a major and important milestone. It can either create the foundation the project needs to maximise benefits realisation or close it down, favouring other projects with more promising business cases.

The benefit-driven change model shows the main activities of the execution phase for the project's three tracks in Figure 7.1. In this third part of the book, I start by addressing the benefits realisation track and what it takes to ensure that we get as much value out of the project as possible. Next, I focus on the specific activities that help us obtain the desired behaviour in the change track, and, along the way, I review the correlation to the tasks in the technical track.

The purpose of the execution phase is to ensure we work towards maximising the benefits realisation in the project.

Figure 7.1 The tasks in the execution phase.

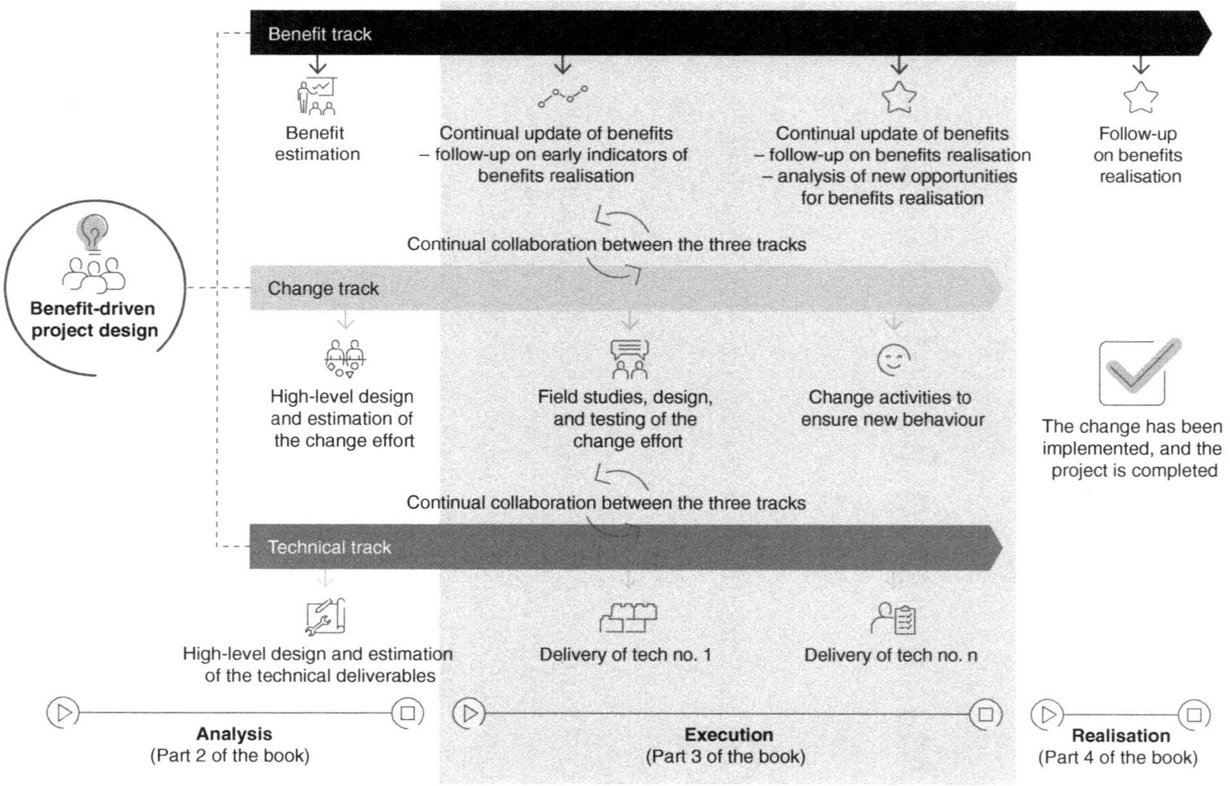

Benefit-driven project design

Benefit track

Benefit estimation

Continual update of benefits
– follow-up on early indicators of benefits realisation

Continual update of benefits
– follow-up on benefits realisation
– analysis of new opportunities for benefits realisation

Follow-up on benefits realisation

Continual collaboration between the three tracks

Change track

High-level design and estimation of the change effort

Field studies, design, and testing of the change effort

Change activities to ensure new behaviour

The change has been implemented, and the project is completed

Continual collaboration between the three tracks

Technical track

High-level design and estimation of the technical deliverables

Delivery of tech no. 1

Delivery of tech no. n

Analysis
(Part 2 of the book)

Execution
(Part 3 of the book)

Realisation
(Part 4 of the book)

The challenge is that, even though we have done our best to prepare and create a good basis for assessing both benefits and costs in the analysis phase, our business case from the analysis phase risks being drained of benefits over time. During the execution phase, we learn more about the benefit potential: changes within and outside our organisation mean that some of the benefits we identified in the analysis phase disappear while others come to light. The typical reasons the benefits may change include changed market conditions (new competitors or new competing products or services), new legislation, or internal changes. Internal changes may consist of changes within the organisation or the benefits realisation of other projects so that these projects either realise the project's benefits or provide the opportunity to realise more benefits in the project. The development of the loss of expected benefits and the project's embracing of new opportunities for benefits realisation during the execution phase is illustrated in Figure 7.2.

The ability to handle the situation where benefits change is more important in some projects than in others. Two parameters determine how much the benefits may change:

- The length of the project.
- The uncertainty associated with realising the individual benefits.[1]

If there is a low degree of uncertainty associated with realising the project's benefits after the analysis phase, the decisive factor for how much the benefits change is the length of the project. The longer a project spans, the more the project's

[1] See Figure 5.3 for estimation methods for various levels of uncertainty related to benefit estimates.

Figure 7.2 The benefits change during the project.

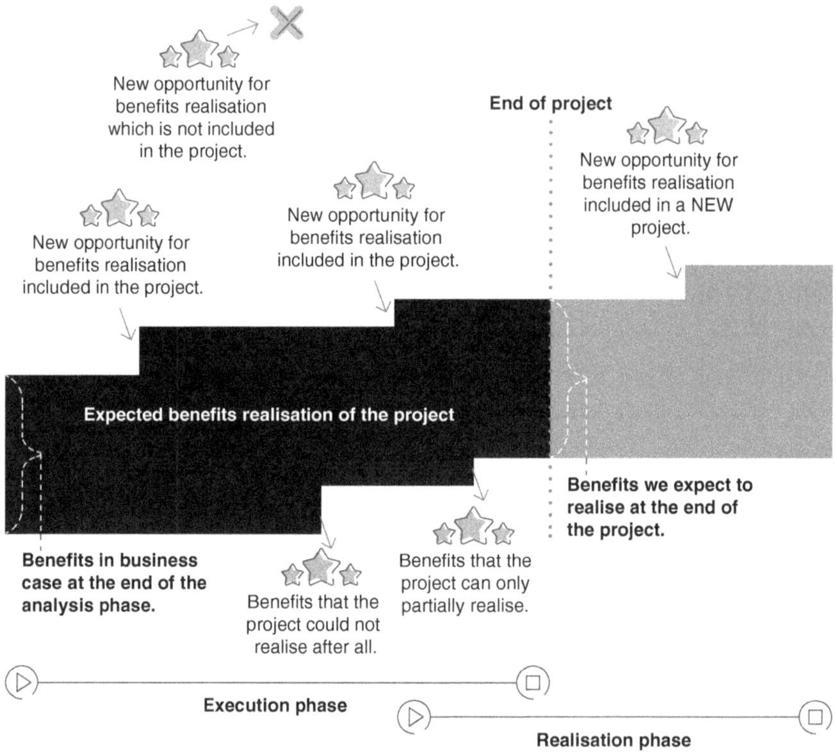

Source: Inspired by Lampel et al. (2003).

benefits are likely to change, as the requirements the project must meet may change over time, just as more opportunities and risks may emerge in a long-term project (Budzier 2014). If there is a high degree of uncertainty associated with the project's benefits, the time factor will, of course, still have the same significance. But in addition to this, the learnings we get from the project during the execution phase will greatly contribute to new knowledge about the expected benefits realisation, thus creating a need to change the project along the way to maximise benefits realisation.

Transparency Enables Decision-making that Maximises Benefits

In order to make decisions that maximise the benefits realisation for a project, we need to create transparency around benefits realisation, risks, new opportunities for benefits realisation, and the costs associated with seizing the opportunities.

Transparency is the methodological prerequisite for us to succeed in realising the full benefit potential. In addition, we must succeed in maximising benefits realisation and make it the foundation for which all small and large decisions in the project are made. The benefit owner and the project manager are not the only ones who should have this in mind: everyone in the project should, because everyone will make decisions that impact how or if the benefits are realised. Maximising benefits realisation should be a regular part of the conversation about the project. Every time we discuss how to maximise benefits realisation, we should also talk about how we minimise the negative benefits that the project may also create. There is almost always a negative benefit in the form of a loss of productivity when we introduce new ways of working. There may also be a loss of down-prioritised customers or reduced employee satisfaction. We need the same transparency about negative benefits and should actively work to minimise them.

In the benefit track, creating the transparency that makes it possible to make decisions that maximise benefits at both the project and the portfolio level depends on whether the project chooses a launch strategy consisting of one or more launches. A launch is the result of the overall efforts to anchor a change in which one or more employee groups have changed behaviour. Thus, a launch creates the prerequisites we expect the benefits realisation requires – and the work to develop a launch usually includes contributions in the form of activities and deliverables from both the technical track and change track. We will start by taking a closer look at projects with one launch.

Tasks in the Benefit Track with One Launch

Although agility and minimum viable product (MVP[2]) are perhaps some of the biggest buzzwords right now, there are still situations where it makes sense to have a launch strategy with only one project launch.

In the benefit track, the approach to this type of project is the same, regardless of whether the technical track uses a delivery model based on a waterfall[3] or a de facto waterfall model from a launch perspective, using, for example, an agile delivery method with many technical releases that does not result in more than one launch to end-users, customers, or citizens. Table 7.1 gives an overview of the tasks during the implementation phase, when this launch strategy should be considered, and the challenges of this strategy.

The optimisation task is based on the benefit map and benefits realisation plan created in the analysis phase. The task is solved by continually collecting information about opportunities

---

[2]The MVP is defined by Ries (2017) as that version of a new product which allows a team to collect the maximum amount of validated learning about customers with the least effort, i.e. learning based on data instead of assumptions. MVP is also used to describe the minimum viable product or service to customers, citizens, or users. Here, MVP is used as an orientation towards continually creating learning and value with a series of value-creating launches for customers, citizens, or users.

[3]In a waterfall model, the project goes through a series of phases until the project is completed and launched in one operation.

Table 7.1 Launch strategy: one launch.

Tasks in the benefit track	Consider the launch strategy when . . .	The challenges of the strategy
Optimisation: Ongoing assessment of the benefits realisability, risks and opportunities for additional benefits realisation. **Analysis** (if applicable): In the event of major changes, it is necessary to repeat the benefit analysis from the analysis phase and prepare a benefit map and a benefit realisation plan as input to a business case for a major change.	• The duration of the project is short. • The level of uncertainty in benefit estimates is low, so the need for feedback from customers, citizens or users is lower. • The project solution can only be used in its entirety. • There are major costs associated with making a step-by-step launch.	• No benefits are realised until the project is completed (possible loss of benefits). • No feedback from customers, end users or citizens to confirm or deny assumptions about benefit realisation. • Difficult to stop as a result of the first two points.

and risks related to benefits and using that information to keep the benefit map and benefits realisation plan up to date. If opportunities to realise new benefits arise, it may be necessary to go back and use the approach from the analysis phase to assess whether to pursue them. The same is true of major changes in the expectations of benefits. We tend to focus more on the risk of losing benefits than on the opportunities to realise more benefits. However, we will need to focus on both elements to avoid a benefit drain from the business case, as shown in Figure 7.2.

The behavioural design principles from Box 7.1 can also be used in the benefit track.

Box 7.1: Make it easy to do the right thing in the benefit track

- **Make it easy to do the right thing.** We can make it easier to work with benefits realisation by having the updated benefit map and the goals for benefits, behaviour, competencies, and deliverables hanging on the wall (physically or virtually) in the places where the project team works and the steering committee meetings take place. The project manager, project group, and benefit owners must constantly be reminded of why we are doing the project. Furthermore, it should be easy to put up ideas on the wall for new possible benefits, new functionality, risks, and issues that may impact the benefits realisation and discuss them accordingly.
- **Make new behaviour the standard for how we work.** Include benefits realisation in the standard agenda for project and steering committee meetings and describe, for example, standard methods for benefit estimation, including the benefits realisation data from completed projects with similar types of benefits.
- **Be specific: describe the visible behaviour.** Make scripts for workshops and project and steering committee meetings, and explain how the tasks in connection with benefit analysis, optimisation, and follow-up can be handled for the most critical roles, including the project manager and benefit owner. An example of behaviour at a steering committee meeting could be that the status, new ideas, risks, and issues (and the consequences they may have for the project) are always reviewed based on the expected impact on the benefit map.

If something happens that can have a significant effect on the benefits, then the benefits, as well as the rest of the project, should be reviewed at once. Otherwise, the review of the project's benefits should take place at a fixed frequency, for example once every quarter. The benefit owner is responsible for monitoring risks and opportunities for the realisation of benefits. However, the practical work of analysing and elaborating on the identified risks and opportunities lies within the project – usually with one of the employees allocated to the project by the benefit owner. The benefit owner often has better prerequisites for identifying new opportunities and risks concerning benefits inside and outside the organisation. At the same time, it is important to place responsibility for monitoring the benefits with the benefit owner to maintain the importance of the project as well as the ownership with them. The benefit owner must ensure that the benefits are realised or that the project is closed in favour of more value-adding projects.

Advantages and Disadvantages of One Launch

The advantages of having only one launch are that the actual project implementation often becomes simpler, quicker, and cheaper. These advantages can outweigh the disadvantages for projects with only a few months' duration or benefits with low uncertainty. In other cases, there may be technical, business, or regulatory complexity, which means that the cost of multiple launches makes it too expensive or impossible to choose a strategy with multiple launches.

The disadvantages of having only one launch are that we must wait for the entirety of the project period to pass before any benefits are realised instead of quickly realising some of the benefits. We thus miss out on the organisational tailwind that quick and validated benefits realisation can provide the project. We also miss the opportunity to get feedback from customers, citizens, or end-users to confirm our assumptions about the cause

Figure 7.3 Benefits realisation in one-launch projects in the execution and realisation phases.

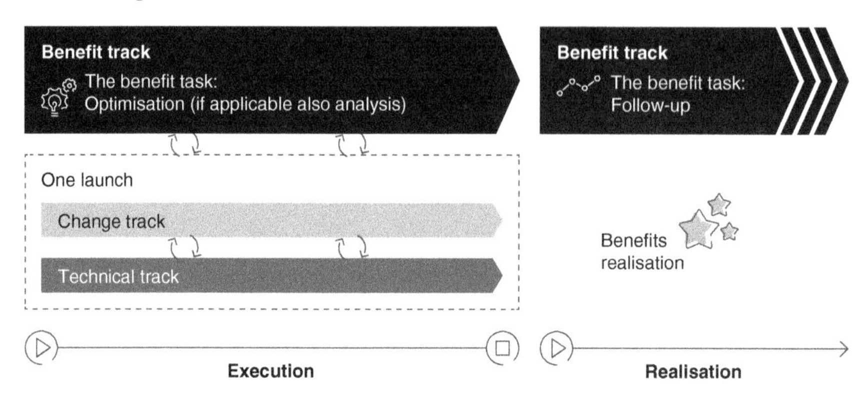

and effect behind the benefits realisation. Therefore, these projects are difficult to close before they are completed as we have not yet realised benefits early in the project, and all the project's resources will usually be wasted if the project is closed. Benefits realisation with one launch is shown in Figure 7.3.

The Follow-up Task

Once the project has completed the technical development and anchored the new behaviour (making it possible to realise the desired benefits), the execution phase ends, closing the project. Figure 7.3 shows that work is being done on both the technical track and change track throughout the execution phase. However, the emphasis is typically on the technical track at the beginning of the execution phase and the change track at the end. Once the execution phase is complete, the project team and project manager move on to the next project. In the realisation phase, there is still a follow-up task that needs to be done.

The follow-up task consists of collecting data and reporting on benefits realisation while matching it with the targets in the benefits realisation plan. Thus, the benefit owner continues to report to the portfolio management with a fixed frequency.

This should be done until we are sure that benefits realisation has been established and there is no need for further reporting. An example of a portfolio management office (PMO) driven process for following up on the benefits is shown in Figure 9.3. The follow-up should be managed at the portfolio level by the PMO, for example, so that the responsibility to follow up on the benefits realisation is an objective part of the organisation. This should also be where the decision is made about when to stop reporting.

Tasks in the Benefit Track for Projects with Multiple Launches

Many organisations choose to break down the development of IT systems, products, services, and their associated changes into smaller steps to test their ability to meet the desired needs, get better feedback, and realise more benefits – faster.

When we break down the technical task and change task into smaller parts in a change project and start working with several launches that include technical development and behavioural change, we also create a need to change the way we work in the benefit track. We will need to determine the benefit for each launch. Therefore, we need to create benefit maps and benefits realisation plans for each launch to be assessed separately. From a benefits realisation perspective, we therefore treat each launch as an independent project. This means that during the execution phase we must do the following steps on an ongoing basis:

- Analyse future launches (as described in Part 2).
- Optimise the ongoing launch.
- Follow up on the benefits realisation from the completed launches.

Thus, the benefit track will take up more time during the execution phase than when the project only has one launch.

Distribution of Tasks

It is still the responsibility of the benefit owner to obtain data so that they can report to the PMO on the benefits that have been realised from completed launches, even if the project is not completed. That task could, in principle, be moved from the project to the business. In practice, the project is committed to following up on value creation and incorporating the learning from the project. Therefore, it makes the most sense that the project is responsible for the operational part of the benefit data collection, while the benefit owner always is responsible for the formal reporting. When the project is completed, the operational part of the data collection is taken over by the benefit owner's organisation. Therefore, the project management and steering committee should have the mandate to reprioritise the content of the ongoing launch without consulting the PMO or portfolio management, unless the changes change the project so radically that it risks affecting other projects' benefits realisation. Table 7.2 provides an overview of the tasks in the benefit track in projects with multiple launches.

The longer a project lasts and the greater the risk associated with the project's benefits, the more effective the launch strategy, either because it ensures a faster and greater realisation of benefits or because the rapid learning leads to faster closing of projects that are not able to realise the expected benefits. Even if the benefits remain unchanged throughout the execution phase, this delivery strategy also provides a real opportunity to assess whether the benefits from the project's next launch can compare with those from investing in another project. The advantages of the launch strategy must be weighed against the possible costs associated with multiple launches, including repeatedly approaching the same employees, asking them to change their behaviour.

Table 7.2 Multi-launch strategy.

Tasks in the benefit track	Consider the launch strategy when . . .	The challenges of the strategy
Analysis: Repetition of the benefit analysis from the analysis phase with the preparation of a benefit map and a benefits realisation plan as input to a business case in the event of new launches and major changes. **Optimisation:** Ongoing assessment of the benefits realisability, risks and opportunities for additional benefits realisation. **Follow-up:** Follow up on whether the benefits from completed launches are realised according to the benefits realisation plan.	• Parts of the benefits realisation can start before the project is finished, thus increasing the overall benefits realisation. • There are valuable learnings to be gained by quickly launching products or services with less functionality or content to customers, citizens or users. • It must be possible to the last project launches against investments in other projects.	• There may be an additional cost associated with each additional launch. • More launches mean that we interrupt employees several times with demands for change of behaviour.

Considerations for Larger Projects

Figure 7.4 shows that the individual launches may vary in duration and either lie in continuation or overlap. Launch 3 can be initiated before launch 2 is completed without much risk if there is great certainty about the benefits. Some organisations choose not to let the change track and technical track run in parallel in larger projects. This means that the change track both prepares change activities (based on what the technical track is currently developing) and implements new behaviours based on what the technical track completed in the previous launch.

Figure 7.4 Maximising benefits realisation with multiple launches.

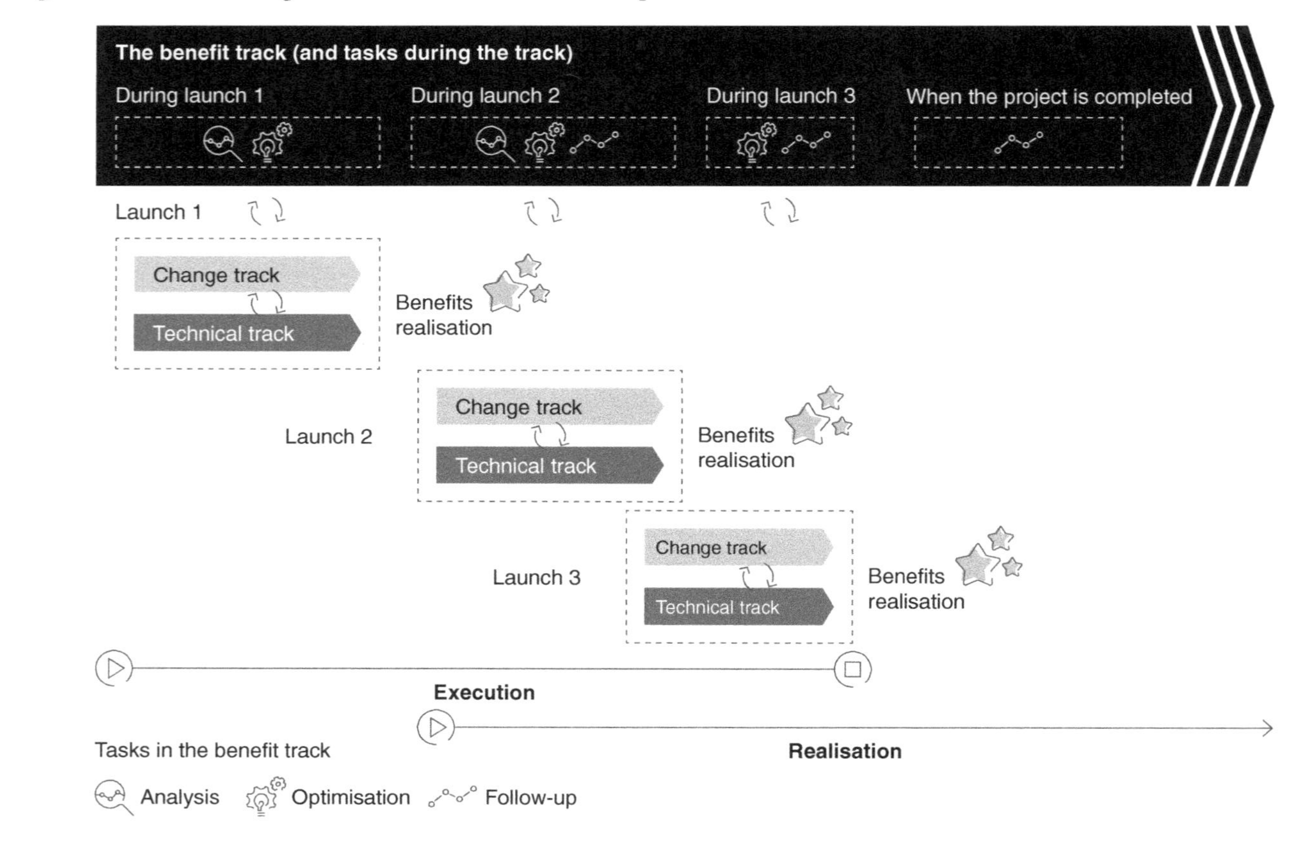

An alternative to the project has been provided for the development task, namely the (fixed) agile team. When we work with development organisations with agile teams, we do not build a new project organisation every time there are new development tasks to solve. Instead, the development tasks are solved by different agile and often specialised teams. The work of benefits realisation in an environment with agile teams can be handled the same way, as shown in Figure 7.4.

Maximising Benefits Realisation with SAFe

'SAFe' stands for scaled agile framework, and in recent years it has been widely used as a method to scale the success that many companies and organisations have experienced when using agile methods in projects.

SAFe, like other agile methods, originated from the need for efficient software development and has proven to be an excellent method to ensure just that. The increased use of SAFe can be seen as a solution to a general challenge: how to produce all types of technical deliverables most efficiently, including hardware and service development. Box 7.2 outlines the SAFe method.

Box 7.2: SAFe in brief[4]

In brief, SAFe is built around the agile team composed of employees with both business and technical competencies. This composition allows the team to design, build, and test their deliverables.

(*Continued*)

[4] SAFe is provided by Scaled Agile, Inc. and described by Leffingwell and Jemillo (2021). The box is inspired by Rytter and Jensen (2018).

(*Continued*)

SAFe does not use the term 'projects' but instead uses a product-lifecycle-based approach, where deliverables often add to an existing product. Deliverables from one agile team may be paired with deliverables from other teams to create a service or functionality of value to the end-user (called a feature).

Team groups: agile release trains

The agile teams are organised around value streams and are gathered in team groups called ARTs (agile release trains), the delivery engine in SAFe. These team groups are set up until there is no more value to be realised, for example when a product is phased out. Thus, these teams can often exist for several years where they create several different services or functionalities (features) that may not even exist at the idea stage yet. The work of these team groups (ARTs) is prioritised at the portfolio level in SAFe. Here, SAFe works with epics, which is defined as major investments that require a separate business case and where the fulfilment of the business case happens through ongoing and early value-creating releases (technical delivery packages) consisting of new features.

The basic hypothesis about value creation in SAFe is that value is automatically created through continual product improvements. As SAFe is a product- and IT-driven method, value is often defined as a product improvement. So, to ensure that SAFe realises benefits when we use the method in situations like change projects where benefits realisation requires changed behaviour in the business, three challenges need to be addressed:

(*Continued*)

(*Continued*)

- **SAFe needs a change track.**
  In many cases, the underlying assumption that delivering a continual stream of product improvements means no need for a change track is not true. To realise the benefit potential of technical features and epics, we should add a change track to build competencies and new behaviours in the business.
- **SAFe can be strengthened with a greater focus on end benefits.**
  The SAFe method has an IT-focused and product-focused 'inside-out' perspective on benefits and often confines itself to defining product KPIs as measures of value instead of end benefits. It also means that ownership is not always created in the business to realise the end benefits.
- **The prioritisation at the portfolio level can be strengthened with input from the benefit track and change track.**
  If we fail to prioritise based on end benefits, and if we omit costs for competency building and behavioural change, in many cases we risk getting the wrong picture of the benefits and what it takes to realise them. Thus, we risk prioritising the wrong things.

Do you work for Spotify or a similar organisation that produces new IT-based services for your customers? And do you not have employees who must adapt to new ways of working as you further develop these services? Then the three challenges are probably not that important to you.

(*Continued*)

(*Continued*)

However, in most organisations, it is too bold to assume that improvements to products or services automatically generate end benefits. Suppose you work in an organisation where the deliverables you produce require new behaviour from your colleagues in citizens services, customer service, sales, marketing, and IT support. In that case, we also need help from a change track. When we use the SAFe method in situations where benefits realisation requires a behavioural change, we are left with almost the same black box in the benefits realisation process as with all the other development models that also have their origin in the production of technical deliverables. We need to change that.

Benefits Realisation in SAFe

To ensure benefits realisation when using SAFe's method of producing technical deliverables, we add benefits realisation the same way we add it to change projects with multiple launches. The trick is to add the benefit track and change track without stripping the SAFe method of the qualities that have made it a commonly used agile method. Therefore, we do not change the agile team.

The development of business cases and the work associated with benefits realisation takes place at the portfolio level in the SAFe method. Therefore, the tasks of analysing, optimising, and following up on benefits realisation are placed at the SAFe method's portfolio level. As no precise end time has been defined for the work in the ART, making benefit analyses, optimisations, and follow-up on benefits remain ongoing tasks. This is managed in the benefit track by an epic owner who can get help from a group of benefit specialists[5] and benefit owners responsible for maturing and developing business cases for new epics and updating business cases for the remaining work of ongoing epics. This work makes it possible to prioritise ongoing epics and the initiation of new ones – or reprioritising the allocation of resources between ARTs, so resources are used where they create the most value.

The tasks of the benefit team consist of:

- Ongoing development of benefit maps and benefits realisation plans for new epics as well as for the remaining parts of ongoing epics.
- Collecting job size or job duration estimates[6] for new and the remaining work of ongoing epics from the agile teams and cost estimates for the change track (often driven by a change team).
- Following up on benefits realisation from epics, which have been completed, and where the change of new behaviour has also been completed.

The benefit team can handle multiple ARTs and, depending on the organisation, handle all ARTs.[7]

---

[5] In SAFe, the epic owner role is responsible for preparing the business case. The tasks in the benefit team have been expanded in relation to the epic owner role, as it includes the entire task of benefit realisation as described in Part 3 as well as collecting data from the change track on the cost of the change.

[6] In SAFe, duration estimates are often made instead of cost estimates, as costs for, for example, salaries for the agile teams in ARTs are assumed to be cost incurred. The cost of the change efforts is not, so here we are still working with cost estimates.

[7] If there are several benefits realisation teams, a governance on prioritising and initiating related epics must be defined so that suboptimisation can be avoided.

Just as the tasks from both the technical track and benefit track have their own teams, the change track also gets its own team. The tasks of the change team consist of:

- Ensuring benefits realisation by ensuring that new behaviour enabled by a technical release is anchored in the business.
- Estimating the size of the change efforts, which together with new or modified technical deliverables (technical releases) will realise benefits.

The change team has a core of change specialists who, in collaboration with first-line managers and ambassadors, help embed new behaviour in connection with the ongoing change efforts or participate in the analysis of upcoming ones. The change team's tasks in making the change in the organisation happen can be as big or much more extensive than the technical task solved by the agile teams in an ART. Therefore, connecting the change team directly to one or maybe two ARTs often makes sense.

Collaboration Across Tracks

Figure 7.5 shows that the benefit team contributes with the data foundation for the ongoing prioritisation of both the ART and the change team's efforts. Realising benefits often means working in parallel in both the change team and the ART to deliver value from an epic in the same way that the change track and technical track work together in change projects.

In Part 1, we used the benefit-driven change model to divide the project into three tracks to visualise the project's many tasks as well as the different skillsets needed to deliver them. The purpose of dividing them into tracks instead of subprojects or subteams is to ensure that the project does not build barriers between

Figure 7.5 Maximising benefits realisation with SAFe.

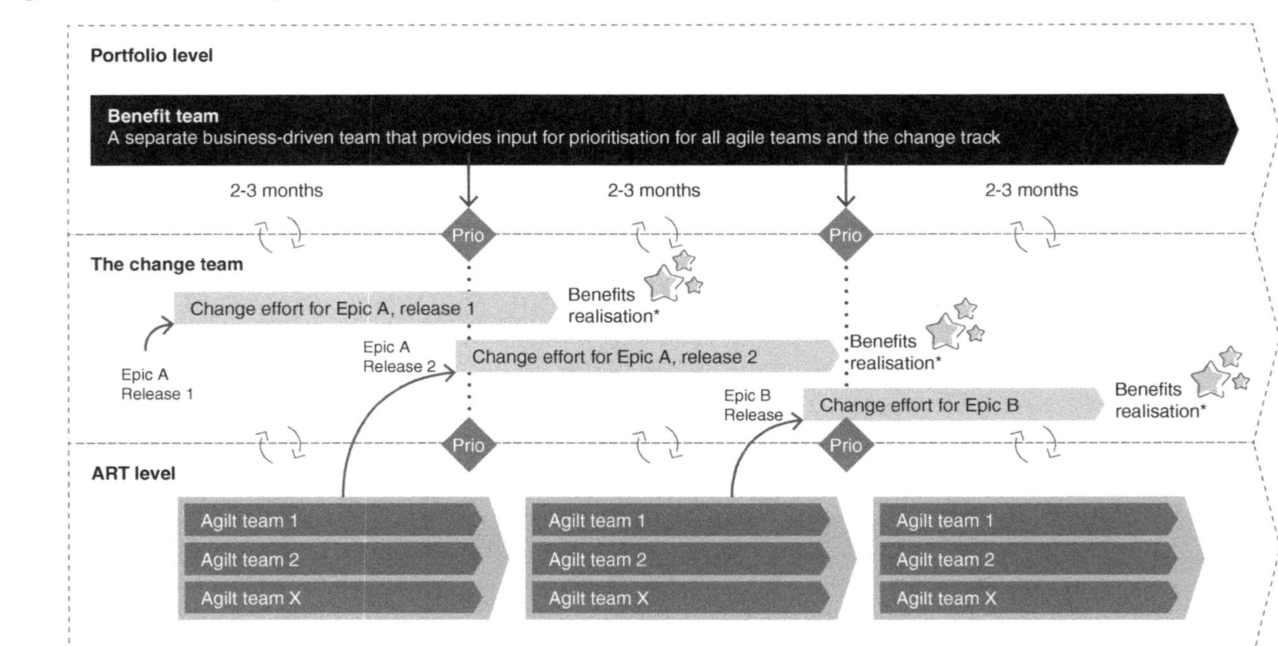

* Benefits realisation can occur on an ongoing basis, as technical releases and organisational launches are not linked to the prioritisation.

project participants who undertake different tasks. When we place all the tasks in separate teams to protect the agile team as the well-oiled delivery engine in the SAFe method, we risk forming silos and weakening the connection between the people working on the technical deliverables and the change efforts. To avoid this, an active effort must be made, for example by letting the change team plan, share learnings, and make demos together with the technical teams.

The Work in the Benefit Track Continues

We will have to work with benefits realisation until the project is completed to ensure we maximise benefits realisation during the execution phase. The task of creating the transparency that makes it possible to make decisions that maximise benefits varies depending on the chosen launch strategy and which delivery model is used in the technical track. But the work continues throughout the project's lifetime. In parallel with the work in the benefit track, work is also being done on the technical track and change track. In Chapter 8, I dive into the change track, where we must help our colleagues change behaviour in the execution phase.

8

Create the Change

In the execution phase, the task in the change track is to ensure that we create the behavioural change needed for us to succeed with benefits realisation and thus the project.

If we have done a good change analysis, we have a well-founded overview of the change at hand, what change activities are required, and, not least, how much the change efforts will cost. We involved managers and key employees from the employee groups who will be affected by the change. In addition to giving us a greater knowledge of the change, the change efforts, and their costs, it has hopefully also helped us to make them advocates for change.

Chapter 7 pointed out that we must expect to learn more about what benefits we are able to realise. And if the benefits change, the need for behavioural change to realise the benefits is likely to do so as well. In the technical track, we will, in many cases, also become wiser about which technical deliverables we can produce and at what cost, and thus which technical barriers to new behaviour we can fully or partly remove. In addition, we also get a better picture of what efforts are needed to create the change in each of the affected employee groups.

In the analysis phase, we have only talked to managers and a few future ambassadors. We have not yet involved larger parts of the employee groups who will be affected by the change. Therefore, it is highly likely that, once we do that, we will learn more about the efforts needed to facilitate the change and thus adjust the plans and estimates we made in the analysis phase.

In the technical track, many organisations have adopted an agile way of thinking and working. They constantly seek to become wiser about their stakeholders' needs and how specific tasks are best solved. The agile way of thinking and working can also be used in the change track. If we borrow the agile terminology, we can see the result of our change analysis as the first minimum viable product (MVP) for the change. The change MVP from the analysis phase includes a preliminary description of the new ways of working, change activities, and a plan for each group of people that need to change behaviour as a result of the project. The first task in the execution phase is to validate our assumptions about the current behaviour and how to make the change happen in the best possible way.

We do this through a field study by seeking out the employees who are about to change behaviour to update our knowledge of their current behaviour, expectations for their reaction to the change, and the organisational and technical barriers we must overcome. With a thought-out field study, we can determine the hooks that can carry the new behaviour – just as we also determine the things we must keep doing or need to stop doing to realise the project's benefits. The knowledge gained from the field study is used to design and develop the change activities for each employee group.

The Change Deliverable Version 1.0

In the design and development part of the change process, several change MVPs are prepared until we finally have a complete change deliverable. The design and development part is partly a design and development exercise and partly an involvement exercise that contributes to creating change. Once we get through it, the finished change MVP will be elevated to be the change deliverable version 1.0. The first part of the change deliverable usually consists of training followed by change support until the new behaviour is in place. In Figure 8.1, 'Initiation of new behaviour' is shown as a point in time between training and change support. This is often also the case if the behavioural change is linked to the release of an important deliverable, for example, when a new IT system is made available. In other cases, the behavioural change begins as soon as we start involving the employees. The change support process continues until the new behaviour is a natural part of how employees work. The change process is shown for both the analysis phase and implementation phase in Figure 8.1.

The change process in the execution phase appears linear, but in many cases it offers a lot of rework as the level of knowledge increases in each of the project's three tracks. In particular, the design and development of the change part and the work to make change happen usually occur as iterative processes, where, with feedback from those who will be part of the change, we adapt our change efforts. The change process is repeated in the execution phase for each of the project launches. For example, if the project has three launches, the process must be completed three times, although the knowledge and relationships we build at the first launch can reduce the change effort at subsequent launches.

Dialogue-based communication and storytelling take place in all parts of the change track. So, the part of communication illustrated as an activity, together with the follow-up on progression, is the development of stories to be told by many managers and ambassadors and the one-to-many communication made about purpose, benefits, and the need for change. How to follow up on progression in the change track is discussed at the end of the chapter.

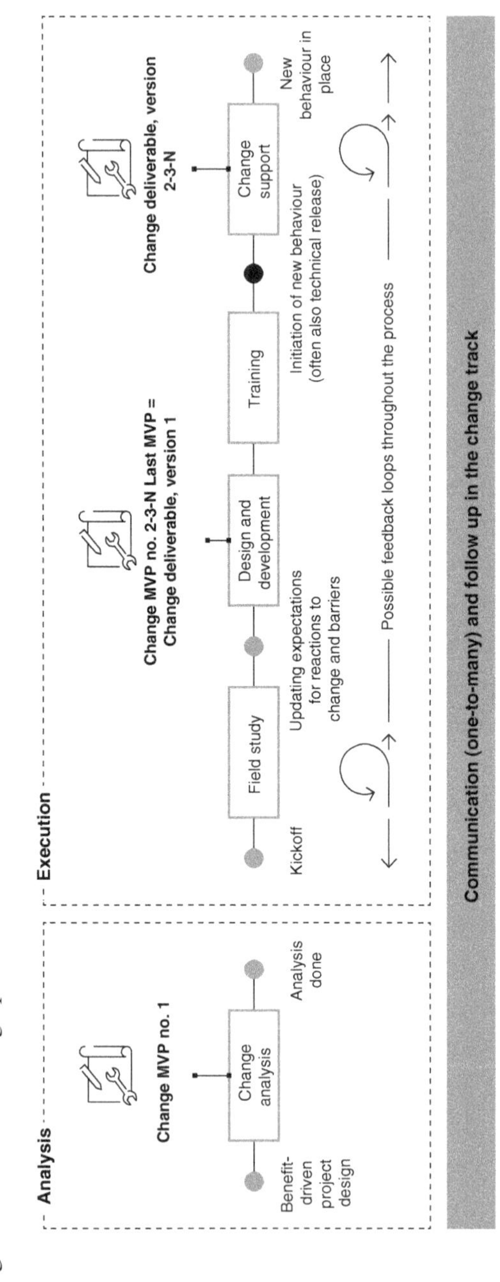

Figure 8.1 The change process.

First-line Managers and Ambassadors

From the beginning of the execution phase, there is a task to identify and mobilise all the first-line managers and ambassadors among the employees we need to bring about change. The need for help from first-line managers and ambassadors will usually increase during the execution phase. We need them to help us handle both positive and negative reactions to change and the work-related challenges we come across when we involve employees during field studies and when we do design and development. We need them to help us get the new behaviour right.[1] Some first-line managers and ambassadors have already been involved in the analysis phase, but often more people must be on board during the execution phase. The mobilisation of first-line managers and ambassadors means that they must be well equipped. That usually includes that they should:

- Be good at explaining to an employee what improvements in performance (benefits) their new behaviours should create.
- Be ready to explain the purpose and benefits of the change project.
- Be prepared to explain what benefits are expected to be in it for them – and the rest of the team.
- Seize any positive interest and use it to help accelerate the change process.
- Invest time for conversations with those who are resisting change or need specific input on how to do their job (ask questions and listen).
- Recognise the challenges that come with changing behaviour.

---

[1] For more inspiration on managing resistance, how to have change conversations, and the importance of the metaphors we use to explain change, see:

- Erichsen (2015): the key to obtaining the best results is found among motivated employees.
- Shaw (2002): *Changing Conversations in Organizations: A Complexity Approach to Change (Complexity and Emergence in Organizations)*.
- Lakoff and Johnson (1981): metaphors we live by.
- Rock (2008): SCARF.
- Loehr and Schwartz (2005): the power of full engagement.

It is the responsibility of the project, possibly with the help of a change specialist, to ensure that first-line managers and ambassadors are equipped to fulfil their new role in facilitating change. That could be in the form of precise formulations about the purpose and benefits of the project and how the change will help the different employees in the long term. It can also be training in understanding resistance and how positive conversations about the change with employees and colleagues should be structured and conducted. The more energy and commitment they can inject into their dialogue with colleagues, the more impact their work has. In the forthcoming sections, we will look at how to approach each part of the change process. We start with field studies and move from there through the process.

The Field Study

The field study is the first step in the change track. Here we validate and build on our assumptions from the analysis phase and lay the foundations for developing new behaviour and the efforts to implement them.

During the field study, our assumptions about the change and the affected employees from the analysis phase are validated and nuanced through much greater involvement and analysis. Our knowledge of behaviour, barriers, and expected change efforts is summarised in some of the deliverables from the change analysis. Therefore, the preparation for the field study is typically based on the overview of current and new behaviour, change activities and activities to build competencies, and lastly the overview of the remaining barriers and their handling (Figure 8.2).

Initially, our priority is to physically visit the employee groups impacted the most by the change. In some cases, the field

Figure 8.2 The basis for the field study for each employee group.

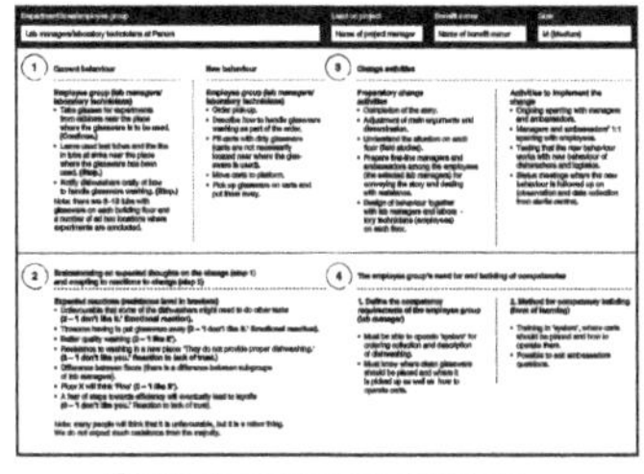

Current and new behaviour, reactions to the change, and efforts in connection with addressing individual barriers (Figure 6.12).

Organisational barriers	Barriers	Handling/requirements	Priority	Owner
Groups	• Different groups of lab managers/laboratory technicians receive different levels of service. • Trust in the quality from the new sterile centre is person-dependent.	• The different groups of lab managers/laboratory technicians should be handled differently. • Special focus on employees who are concerned about quality. • Use the most positive ones as examples or pilots.	• High • High • N/A	Project: PM name Steerco: Benefit owner name
Organisation	• The six sterile centres need to be merged. • A logistics function for handling the transport of glassware between the places of use to the sterile centre needs to be established.	• Close five sterile centres. • Prepare the largest sterile centre for handling dishes from the entire faculty. • Build logistics function.	• High (not MVP) • High (not MVP) • High	Project: PM name Steerco: Primary benefit owner's name
Norms and culture	• Standardisation measures at the faculty have in the past been met with scepticism and resistance.	• Great involvement of each of the individual employee groups in relation to the size of the change. • Invest in making it as easy as possible for lab managers/laboratory technicians.	• High • Medium	Project: PM name Steerco: Primary benefit owner's name

Technical barriers	Barriers	Handling/requirements	Priority	Owner
Technical and physical framework	• A system for ordering and communicating with dishwashers. • Lack of room for carts on several floors. • Carts with dirty glassware are only allowed in specific lifts.	• A system for ordering and communicating with dishwashers is to be made. Note: The MVP can be a marker and a laminated piece of paper • Create space for the carts on each floor. • Possible safety issues must be examined, and agreements on use of lifts must be in place.	• High • (IT-system not MVP) • Medium • High	Project: PM name Steerco: Primary benefit owner's name
Processes	• Ordering and order handling process. • Process/work procedure for purchasing new glassware.	• A process/work procedure for ordering and order handling must be made. • Process/work procedure for purchasing new glassware must be made.	• High • Medium (not MVP)	Project: PM name Steerco: Primary benefit owner's name
Products and services	• The types of glassware available need to be defined. • The service for picking up and delivering glassware needs to be defined, as well as whether there is an emergency service.	• Involvement of individual employee groups to determine selection. • Involvement of individual groups to determine needs.	• High (not MVP) • High (not MVP)	Project: PM name Steerco: Primary benefit owner's name

The identified organisational and technical barriers and how to handle them (Figure 6.15).

study becomes far too extensive if we are to involve all affected employees. In those cases, the priority is to identify which subset of an employee group can be representative and then limit the field study to that subset. Box 8.1 gives an overview of the most commonly used methods for field studies.

Box 8.1: Field studies

There are several different methods for doing field studies. A combination of several methods usually provides the best result. First, you choose which methods to use for each employee group and which employees to involve. Along the way, hypotheses about the current behaviour, possible reactions, and barriers to change from the analysis phase are validated and detailed. Figure 8.3 details the various field studies.

You may want to reuse questions from the change workshop that resulted in the posters in Figure 8.2.

(Continued)

(Continued)

Figure 8.3 Field studies.

Walk-along interviews
An ethnographic interview captures locally anchored knowledge and meaning from an activity, as the interview is conducted in an everyday context while the activity is taking place. This provides an opportunity to explore specific aspects of an activity and ask in-depth questions about processes that you are not yet an expert on.
It is possible to ask for help in understanding the current behaviour.

Video ethnography
Visual recordings are an effective tool in an analysis as they enable you to notice details by observing the target group. Reviewing a video more than once also reveals additional knowledge about current behaviours and barriers.

Participant observation
How well do we really understand the employees we have selected as sources of information? And do we really know what it is like to be in their shoes? Suppose you put yourself into the environment where the employees work and (to the best of your ability) give yourself the experiences that employees have. In that case, we get a more complete picture of the employees' behaviour and the barriers they experience in their daily work.

Shadowing
Shadowing an employee during their daily routines can provide knowledge about their most important and value-adding activities. It can be an excellent way to get valuable information from the employee through observation. However, you need to be aware of bias, e.g. the Hawthorne effect (the possibility that people behave differently because they know they are being observed).

Expert interviews
A task review with a person who is an expert in the area or process in which the current behaviour exists can highlight the current behaviour's challenges for the employee group solving the task and for other employee groups. Likewise, the expert can highlight opportunities by new behaviours that may result in improvements for this or other employee groups.

Choice of Method

When choosing our method to learn more about what happens in the employee groups, we must be clear about what we want to know. For example, if we want to understand the rationale behind the current behaviour and at the same time be able to identify where the employee group experiences frustration or success, a walk-along interview is the right choice. Being able to stop an employee while they are working to ask about their reasons for doing what they are doing gives us valuable insight into their underlying motives. The opposite is true for shadowing, where our attention is aimed at the employee group's interaction and context. Here we choose not to interrupt. Instead, we pay attention to the work process, visible barriers, and help mechanisms that our change must remedy or build on. Therefore, the choice of method is about being clear about what we are interested in getting to know more about and how it can be uncovered in the best possible way.

Validating Assumptions

If, for practical or economic reasons, it is not possible to physically meet all employee groups or representative parts of them, we must, to a greater extent, base our efforts to increase our knowledge about current behaviour and the reasons for it on already existing data. By supplementing field studies with quantitative data, we can hopefully gain the knowledge we need. We rarely have access to the data ourselves, so usually, we have to go out to collect it. The first-line managers and ambassadors we have already worked with during the change analysis are often a good place to start. If they do not have access to the data themselves, they can typically point us in the right direction. If there are other managers or employees we need to get in touch with, they will, in many cases, be able to act as ambassadors afterwards. The field study and data collection can thus be the first opportunity to mobilise and involve more of the managers and future employee ambassadors we will need to make change happen.

When we seek to validate our assumptions from the change analysis, there are a few attention points worth having in mind when you have your dialogue with managers and employees who have not yet been involved in the project:

- Be ready to be proved wrong – pay attention to your solution bias.[2] If we get statements or data that do not match our assumptions from the analysis phase, be careful not to reject the new input with 'good arguments'. Instead, information contrary to assumptions from the analysis phase must be thoroughly verified.
- Be ready to compromise. Not all knowledge we are looking for is at hand, and it may require a major investment to collect and process data. We are looking for a reasonable validation of the assumptions made in the analysis phase and not 100% certainty.
- Build on the relationship with those you meet. You will probably need to use these relationships during the remainder of the project and maybe even afterwards.

There is a great deal of risk involved in working with incorrect assumptions about current behaviour. Therefore, the investment in understanding employees through the field study and other data is central when designing new behaviour, the change activities, and the technical solution. Once these efforts have made us wiser, the next step is to design and develop our approach to create the change and the tools we need. In other words, we are building the next change MVP with the new knowledge from the field study.

[2] Solution bias is a person's tendency to adhere to their own understanding of the solution and reject new (conflicting) information by arguing that it is invalid. That is one of the main reasons we miss the mark in our change efforts (Robertson and Kesselheim 2018).

Design and Development of the Change

After the field study, the development of the change efforts occurs in parallel with the development of the technical deliverables. Technical MVPs are tested in combination with the testing of possible change efforts in the change track.

At this point in the process, changing behaviour and developing the technical deliverables are intricately linked. Each time we get new knowledge in one track, it usually has consequences for the other. Learning loops for the technical track and change track, respectively, consist of a Build–Measure–Learn cycle, as illustrated in Figure 8.4. The figure shows how the technical MVPs are tested to assess how well they contribute to dealing with the technical barriers to change. The content of 'Build' in the technical track is determined by what technical deliverables the employees need to help them change behaviour.

After we measure the impact of the technical MVPs, and thus learn more about how best to reduce technical barriers, that

Figure 8.4 Learning cycles for the development of technical deliverables and the change efforts.

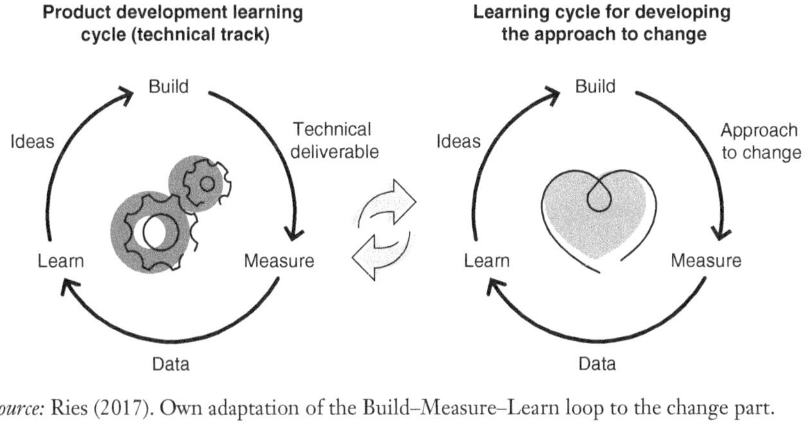

Source: Ries (2017). Own adaptation of the Build–Measure–Learn loop to the change part.

knowledge is used in designing new versions. The technical MVPs often evolve from simple mock-ups to increasingly resembling the technical deliverable that colleagues, citizens, or customers receive as the final product. If we discover new technological possibilities or limitations along the way, they affect the learning cycle for change and can make the change efforts both greater and lesser.

Description of the Change Deliverable

When we start working with MVPs and learning cycles in a change context, we can see the result of our work with the design and development of change efforts as a series of change MVPs that, like technical deliverables, evolve through a series of interconnected learning loops. Upon completing the design and development task, the most recently tested and approved version of the change MVP becomes the first version of the change deliverable. It often consists of:

- Script for new behaviour (see Box 8.2).
- MVP for the technical deliverables.
- Training approach.
- First-line managers' and ambassadors' coaching and influence of the members of the employee group.
- Support for first-line managers and ambassadors (backstage leadership; see Figure 6.10).
- Method for follow-up on progress.

Developing the change MVP often benefits from or requires interaction with the employees affected by the change. The time spent with those who need to change their ways of working not only gives us a better idea of how best to make it easy and attractive to embrace the new behaviour: it also creates much greater ownership of the change, as they help design their new workday through input to both the new behaviour and the technical deliverables that will support it. The time spent on design and development early on in the change process is often well spent, as the work of providing subject matter support and handling reactions to change later on will most likely decrease. This is partly due to the ownership we get from employees who have participated in designing their own future workday, but it is also from the greater understanding we get about our colleagues' ways of working and the opportunities to improve them.

As the designer of the change, it is essential to remember that, no matter how big the change is for the organisation, the change will always be experienced in a microcosm by all the people who must go through the change. The change for the individual employee can always be boiled down to the fact that, in a specific situation, Jane will tomorrow do X instead of Y. Therefore, we make a script for the new behaviour of the employee groups that will significantly change their ways of working.

Box 8.2: Script for new behaviour: a practical guide

The script for the new behaviour is an important part of the change MVP, and it is a format we use to describe new behaviour in the execution phase. The script is made at a workshop focusing on a specific group of employees. The workshop is typically done for the employee groups

(Continued)

(Continued)

who are going through the most notable change. Please note that this workshop requires enough knowledge to break down future behaviour into smaller parts. We usually have that knowledge after the field study and the development of the first technical MVP(s).

The desired outcome of the workshop

- New behaviour described for a specific group of employees that is as easy and attractive as possible from the employees' point of view.
- Breaking down the desired behaviour into smaller parts so that, for each part, we can make the new behaviour easier to perform or make the unwanted behaviour more difficult to perform.
- Increased ownership and motivation for participating first-line managers, ambassadors, and employees.

Before the workshop

Before the workshop, there are several tasks to be addressed:

- Mobilisation and preparation of first-line managers and ambassadors.
- Mobilisation of employees who are to participate in the workshop but have not yet been involved in the project. This includes having conversations with employees who might have negative emotional and trust-related reactions to the change.
- Technical MVP to be used as a demo.
- Planning of the facilitation, including role distribution at the workshop.

(Continued)

(Continued)

During the workshop

The standard workshop agenda, 'Script for new behaviour' (Figure 8.5), looks like this:

- Welcome and purpose (5–10 minutes).
- Recap of the benefits we need to realise as well as the employee group's role in realising the benefits, for example by reviewing the benefit map (10 minutes).
- Workshop, part 1: breakdown of behaviour in steps (30–40 minutes).

An example

In the Nykredit Business Bank case (see Chapter 3), when the benefit ('An adviser has succeeded in getting a new business customer') the new behaviours should deliver has been identified, the first question could be:

'What behaviour is required for an adviser to succeed in getting a new business customer?'

Answer: 'The adviser has helped the customer sign a contract.'

Next question: 'What behaviour is demonstrated before the adviser helps the customer to sign a new contract?'

Answer: 'The adviser has a dialogue with the customer about the value of new products.'

Next question: 'What behaviour is demonstrated before we review product benefits with the customer?'

(Continued)

(Continued)

Answer: 'The adviser contacts potential customers with high expected profitability whom the adviser expects will greatly benefit from the products the Nykredit Business Bank has to offer.'

This breakdown continues until the behaviour is no longer related to the very task of selling to potential Business Bank customers. Each step is written on a yellow index card.

- Workshop, part 2: we take each step and clarify how to make it either easier to do the right thing (grey card) or more challenging to have unwanted behaviour (green card) or how desired behaviour can be made more attractive (pink card) (30–45 minutes).
- Wrap up and next step (15 minutes).

Figure 8.5 Script for new behaviour: an example of output from the workshop.

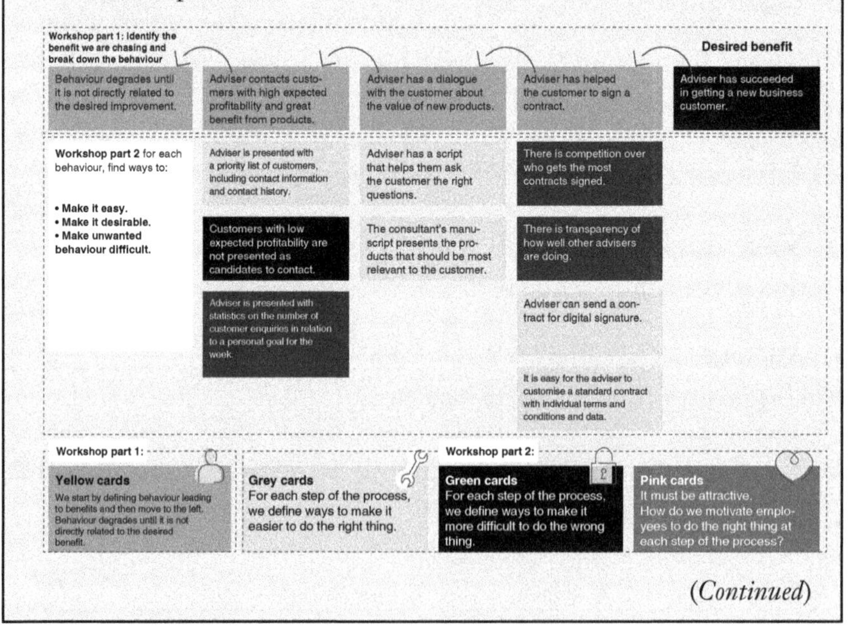

(Continued)

(*Continued*)

Format	Workshop
Materials	Benefit map (for example poster or PowerPoint) Coloured index cards or Post-its, markers, and sticky tack (if physical workshop)
Technical deliverables	Technical MVP (prototypes) and/or (simulation of) new physical environment
Duration	1½–2 hours
Participants	First-line managers and ambassadors, other employees, the project manager, and/or the change manager
Result	The manuscript for new behaviour for an employee group

Source: Inspired by Heath and Heath (2007). Application to practice: Mads Herskind and Rasmus Rytter.

Testing the Change MVP

Just as we test what we develop in the technical track, we also need to test the MVPs we make to design and develop the change deliverable. Testing and measuring change MVPs should be done in an environment as close to reality as possible. It can be on the floor of a production hall, at the reception, the office, or where the group of employees works. The broader the involvement, the greater the ownership. Suppose we have a design and development strategy that involves several MVPs. In that case, it is possible to increase the number of people involved as the quality of the change MVP increases. The test can also be divided into a training and execution part, and there is not only one fixed format for tests that works. The test is usually done as a simulation, and one way to approach the test is the Testing the change efforts workshop shown in Box 8.3.

Box 8.3: Testing the change efforts workshop

The workshop for testing the change efforts is conducted once or several times before 'Initiation of new behaviour' (see Figure 8.1) until the employees' reaction to the simulation is satisfactory and we have created the benefits we aimed to realise.

Desired workshop result

- Test the change MVP, which consists of a script for new behaviour, MVP for technical deliverables, and planned training and change activities.
- Get input to customise technical MVP and change MVP as well as any new behaviours (described in the script for new behaviour).
- Deal with as much resistance to change as possible before the actual launch.

Before the workshop

Before the workshop, there are several tasks to be addressed:

- Mobilise and prepare first-line manager(s) and ambassadors.
- Conversations with employees who are likely to show resistance to the change.
- Create an environment with the physical environment under which new behaviours must take place (if possible).

(*Continued*)

(Continued)

- Plan the facilitation, including role distribution at the workshop.

During the workshop

The standard agenda for the test the change MVP workshop looks like this:

- Welcome, purpose of the workshop, and agenda (10 minutes).
- The desired purpose and benefits (10 minutes).
- Learning points from field studies as well as from the design and development part of the change efforts (10 minutes).
- Presentation of proposals for new behaviour (15 minutes).
- Test/simulation of new behaviour with technical MVP (1–2 hours).
  - Feedback and input for improvements.
  - Adjusting the design:
    - Changes in behaviour;
    - Requests for technical deliverables.
  - New test (if any).
- Recap, possible planning of new test and next steps (15 minutes).

Once the test/simulation has been completed, we round off the workshop with learning points, requests for changes to the technical MVP, and what changes we need to look into.

(Continued)

(*Continued*)

After the workshop

- Adjusting script for new behaviour.
- Communicating wishes to the next technical MVP and change MVP.
- Possible planning of the next test.
- Update the overall change schedule if needed.

Format	Workshop
Materials	The benefit map to present the project (for example poster or PowerPoint), learning points summarised (for example coloured index cards or PowerPoint), new behaviour, preferably visualised (demo in conjunction with technical MVP and simulated conversation with a customer or the like)
Technical deliverables	Technical MVP (prototypes) and (simulation of) new physical environment
Duration	2–3 hours
Participants	Manager(s) and employees, project manager, and/or change manager
Result	Feedback on change MVP and technical MVP, early handling of resistance, and mobilisation of ownership among contributing managers and employees to the change

It is best to test training and simulate the script for behaviour in combination with the technical MVP. Training the ambassadors' abilities to assist the employees can also be tested via simulation, just as is the case for testing the ambassadors' abilities to deal with resistance to change. If the follow-up on progress in the change consists of following up on data, for example by measuring the employees' use of a new IT system, it should also be tested whether the data can be produced. If the follow-up consists of observations of new behaviours, we should check that we are clear about which parts of the behaviour script behaviour we want to follow up on.

Once our behavioural MVP passes the test, it becomes our change deliverable version 1.0. We are now ready to take the next steps in the change process that covers training and change support.

Training, Change Support and Follow-up on Progress

Training and change support – the last parts of the change process – are where we put in our final change efforts in order to help our colleagues change behaviour.

In projects where only a few employees are affected by the change, it is in some cases possible to involve everyone in the design and development part of the change process. In other cases, a considerable portion of the affected employees have not been directly involved but may have only received information about the change at a meeting or in a one-on-one session with their manager.

Although training and change support are shown as two separate activities in Figure 8.1, the two tasks often overlap. As soon as the training begins, we must be ready to deal with reactions to the change, as many have either not been given the opportunity to express positive or negative reactions – or because this is the first time they are presented with the details of what the project is about and how it will affect their ways of working.

The training task itself must provide the employees with the new competencies needed to solve their tasks in the new way. The list of new competencies we identified for each employee group in the change analysis has been updated during the 'design and development' part, just as the choice of training method (traditional classroom training, e-learning, etc.) might also have been changed.

Distribution of Roles

In cases where most of those who need to change behaviour have not previously been particularly involved in the project, the training and change support efforts usually consist of putting the change deliverable into use. We deliver training based on the script for new behaviour and technical MVP and let the first-line managers and ambassadors provide the subject matter support and handling of resistance to change that is necessary. The project's task is to provide the backstage leadership needed, often in the form of coaching with first-line managers and ambassadors or providing concrete support for change activities, for example preparing or facilitating workshops.

The project manager or the change manager responsible for the change track is also responsible for continually collecting feedback and suggestions for improvements in cooperation with employees, line managers, and ambassadors, as shown in Figure 6.10. Finally, the project manager or the change manager also follows up on progress, as knowledge of progress in the change track is key to managing the project.

Follow-up on Progress in the Change Track

How far have we come, how long before we finish, and what will it end up costing? These are questions that many organisations ask their IT or construction project managers. That is not enough.

These are, of course, also questions we must ask those responsible for the change track and to which we should expect to get a satisfactory answer. Measuring progress on behavioural change is usually more complicated than measuring progress on a project developing an IT system or building a bridge. To measure progress, we need to have a common language for how an employee group's change of behaviour typically takes place and methods to provide an actual estimate of what progress has been made. We can use the term 'tipping points' to create the common language, which describes key points in a change process. The first tipping point occurs when about 20% of employees have begun to adopt the new behaviour, indicating that the remaining employees cannot ignore the change. Our change efforts will support the adaption of the new behaviour to the rest of the group. The more trust the first 20% of employees enjoy from the rest of the group, the easier the new behaviour will spread (Herrero 2011). See Figure 8.6.

Once the first tipping point is reached, you need to get the people with a wait-and-see attitude on board (Maxwell 2013).[3] The second tipping point is defined by the fact that now the change is no longer something we are looking for but something we do every day – even if there may be some left whose behaviour has not yet changed (Gladwell 2000). The second tipping point represents a critical mass, i.e. the point at which the new behaviour no longer risks being rolled back. That occurs when about 70% of the employee group has changed behaviour.

[3] And see Part 2.

Figure 8.6 The tipping point for changing behaviour.

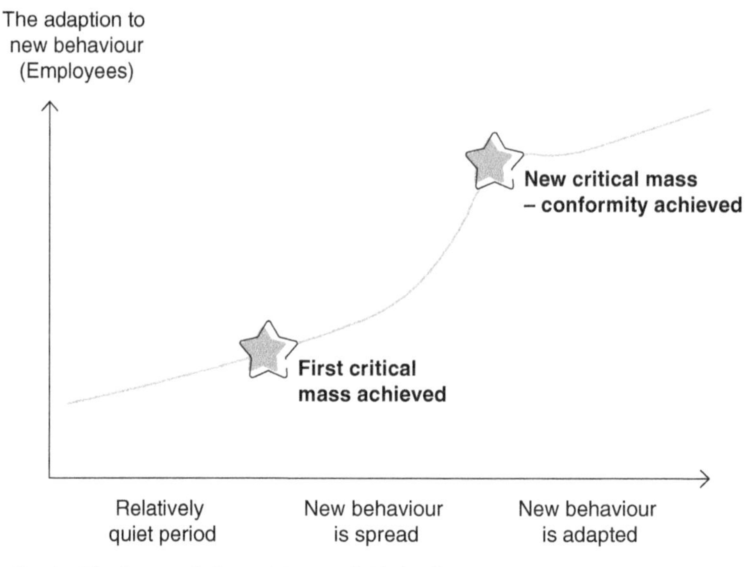

Source: Inspired by Ryan and Gross (1943) and Gladwell (2000).

In order to answer the question of how progress in the change track is coming along, there are four methods we can use (see also Part 2):

1. Behavioural data provided by IT systems.
2. Questionnaire – ask about behaviour.
3. Interviews.
4. Observations of behaviour.

Data Is King, but It Cannot Stand Alone

If we can extract data from an IT system, it often gives an accurate picture of how far we are, for example transitioning to using a digital solution. Data should always be part of the assessment of progress when that sort of data can be obtained. But whether the data is available or not, you need to supplement it with first-hand

Figure 8.7 The energy bar.

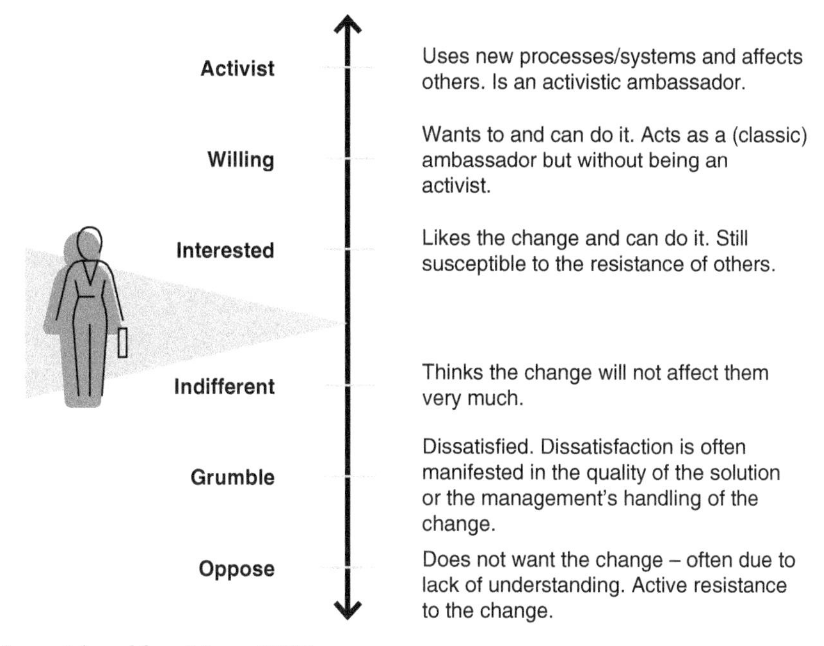

Source: Adapted from Maurer (2021).

impressions from the employee groups where the change occurs. Those impressions come from either the first-line managers or ambassadors who help us make the change happen.

When we meet during the project to discuss progress and what it takes to reach the desired behaviour, it is often good to ask our ambassadors a few questions. They may have to consider where the employee group is in relation to tipping points, where each of their colleagues or employees are located on the energy bar in Figure 8.7, which activities we should put more effort into, and which should be scaled down.

The energy bar reflects the reactions to change and is a way of talking about what reactions to change we must handle to succeed with our change efforts. Not all employees have to be activists or act as (classic) ambassadors. Often, it is enough to have a small group of activists and ambassadors, while the rest just need to get above 'indifferent' on the scale. The important thing is to create a shared picture of the employee group, how far each employee needs to move, and what it will take. This discussion occurs between the project manager or the change manager and the first-line managers and ambassadors (perhaps aided by a change specialist). Together, they find out what needs to be done and what support the first-line managers and ambassadors may need. Once a month, the conversation should also result in an updated estimate to complete the change effort to give the project manager an idea of how much time the change manager, first-line managers, ambassadors, and employees need to get to the finish line.

Visualisation of the Progress

One way to make it easier to keep track of progress in the change track is to use some of the tools your organisation already uses in the technical track. A good example is the use of Kanban boards to visualise progress.[4] Figure 8.8 shows a Kanban board used to follow up on the progress in implementing agile ways of working in a company. Behavioural user stories are written on coloured index cards on the far left under 'To Do', detailed in a series of tasks (specific behaviour) written on Post-its. Each Post-it containing a task is placed as 'To Do', 'Doing', or 'Done', depending on how far along the employee group (team) is in anchoring the new behaviour. The Kanban board can easily be used, even if you do not use user stories as a format to describe behaviour, for

[4] Kanban boards are tools that help to visualise tasks, limit the number of tasks in progress, and maximise the productivity of the project team. The leftmost column often represents groups of tasks that together make up the project team's backlog (total set of tasks). When a task is placed on the board, it moves through the workflow until it is done.

Figure 8.8 Behaviour tracked in a Kanban board.

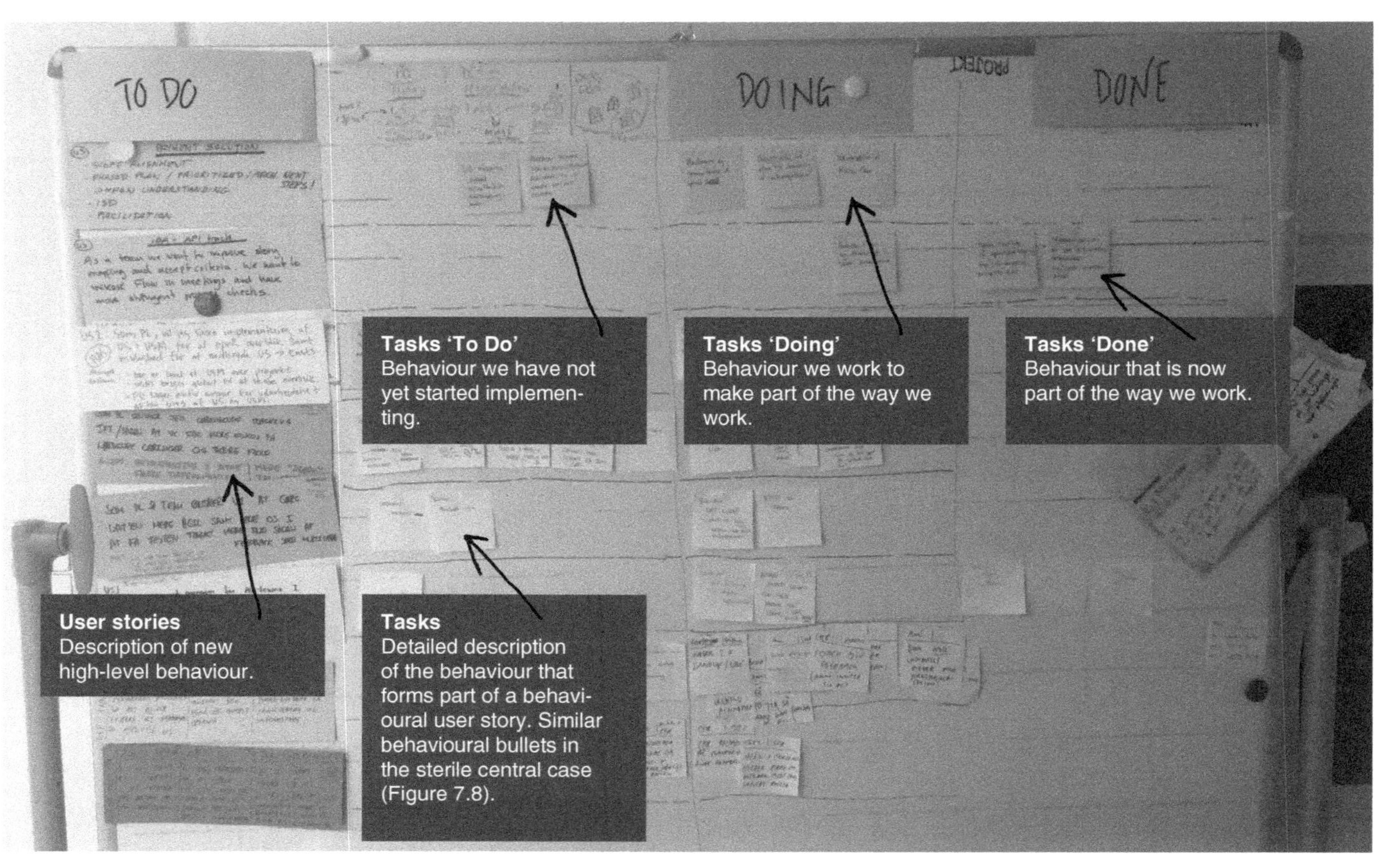

Source: Whiteboard design and photo: Christian Mark Christensen.

example by placing each employee group in a row where the specific behaviour we want to implement is described on Post-its.

The energy bar and the Kanban board can be used individually or together. Both tools create an overview of where we are in changing behaviour and can strengthen the conversation about how best to take the next step towards the new behaviour. At the same time, it is the starting point for estimating the efforts ahead of us for each employee group.

The Benefit Track Lives On

When the new behaviour has become the natural way of working, we have delivered what we set out to do in the change track. The goal of the execution phase is to ensure we lead the project in a way that helps us realise as many benefits as possible. When we have been through the change process in Figure 8.1, we have reached the point where the project has created the prerequisites for realising benefits and thus also created the prerequisite for closing the project.

After the project is closed, there are still tasks to be done in the benefit track – not by the project but by the benefit owner. They will keep reporting on benefits realisation until the portfolio management office (PMO) function is satisfied that the benefits are here to stay. In addition, the new work routines must become part of the organisation's operational management so that the new behaviour and the new performance improvements are further developed as part of the continual improvements of the organisation's operations. In Part 4, I describe what it takes to scale the use of the benefits realisation method from the project level to the entire project portfolio.

Part IV

Scaling Benefits Realisation

9

Scaling Benefits Realisation to the Project Portfolio

Parts 2 and 3 of the book have focused on the ability to realise benefits from a single change project. In this chapter, I focus on how to scale benefits realisation to the entire organisation.

To succeed in unleashing the entire organisation's benefit potential, scaling the use of benefits realisation to the entire portfolio is required. We need to utilise the data we generate in the projects' benefit track, change track, and technical track to ensure better project prioritisation and thus maximisation of benefits realisation for the entire portfolio. The new ways of working with benefits realisation and change in projects thus become our enablers for working with benefits realisation at the portfolio level.

If we are to maintain project managers' and benefit owners' new ways of working with benefits realisation and change in the long term, it is imperative that we are able to further develop the methods and continually adapt them to the needs of the organisation. Furthermore, we must ensure competency building and support for new project managers and benefit owners, so that future colleagues will also use the new methods. This is where the portfolio office, also called the PMO (portfolio management office), comes into play.

The functions or services provided by the PMO in an organisation vary greatly, depending on the organisation's project maturity and what services the organisation's stakeholders assess they need from the PMO (Thomas and Mullaly 2008). Figure 9.1 illustrates the typical services of the technically driven PMO and the add-ons that are often included if the PMO is given the responsibility of ensuring the maximisation of benefits realisation at the portfolio level. The services can be divided into four categories: portfolio management and governance, capacity management, performance management, and best practice support.

It is important to see the individual services as building blocks that can be adapted to the organisation's needs or omitted if provided in another part of the organisation. They must be built up step by step at a pace aligned to the organisation's project maturity and budget. It is important to emphasise that the quality of the services provided by the PMO in many cases depends on other of their services because they support each other and are closely linked. Therefore, organisations with an extensive portfolio of change projects need most of their services from the PMO to maximise benefits realisation across the project portfolio. At the same time, the PMO, like any other internal service function, should be run with as little cost as possible. Below I will go through the PMO's four main services.

Portfolio Management and Governance

The number-one service on the list in most PMOs is facilitating management's prioritisation of the organisation's project portfolio with the help of a basis for decision-making prepared by the PMO.

Figure 9.1 Services in the benefit-driven PMO.

Category
Portfolio management and governance
Capacity management
Performance management
Best practice support
Services
Facilitation of portfolio prioritisation
Ownership and development of project and portfolio management
Support for strategy development process
Capacity management for doing technical development
Capacity management for creating change in behaviour
Planning based on the organisation's ability to handle change
Capacity management for working with benefits realisation
Technically oriented project reporting and follow-up
Follow-up on behavioural change
Benefit follow-up
Ensuring changes to budgets as a result of benefits realisation
Support for innovation, idea generation, project start-ups, and scrutiny
Technical: ownership and development of processes and tools. Training and support for project managers
Change: ownership and development of processes and tools. Training and support for project managers
Benefits realisation: ownership and development of processes and tools. Training and support for project managers
Colour codes
Services related to technical deliverable production
Services related to behavioural change
Services related to benefits realisation

Source: Inspired by Axelos and Roden (2013).

The basis for decision-making is crucial for making the right decisions on how to develop the organisation. Therefore, the quality of it is also vital to the organisation's benefits realisation. From the outside, the facilitation of portfolio prioritisation may appear similar in a technically driven and benefit-driven PMO. Still, the quality of this service depends to a large extent on the other services provided by the PMO. To run a successful benefit-driven PMO, we need the projects to deliver realistic estimates for benefits realisation and the resources it takes to succeed with the benefit track, change track, and technical track. We need:

- The three tracks to be reflected in our capacity management.
- The benefit estimates to be credible and updated regularly.
- To establish a process for collecting and processing data.

When all the above is in place, we can provide the organisation's management with a basis for prioritisation that makes it possible to maximise the benefits realisation at the portfolio level and ensure that we are not trying to realise the same benefits in multiple projects. Thus, the facilitation of management's prioritisation of the portfolio in the benefit-driven PMO provides management with the best possible basis for making decisions that maximise benefits realisation.

An Effective Implementation Platform

In addition to facilitating the portfolio prioritisation, the PMO should also own and develop the organisation's project and portfolio governance (including the project model) and the roles and responsibilities of project and portfolio management. The combination of being responsible for both portfolio prioritisation and governance makes the PMO an effective implementation platform for new methods and behaviours. The PMO can be used to create a demand in the organisation for new project behaviour – something that can also come in useful in the implementation of, for example, a structured approach to benefits realisation and change. Finally, the PMO often helps apply the strategy to a number of projects or programmes by ensuring a clear and continuous link between strategy and portfolio – and possibly by supporting the strategy development itself.

By making the PMO benefit-driven, we create better incentives for the benefit owners. The technically driven portfolio management's lack of transparency of benefits realisation and costs of change, combined with a lack of follow-up on benefits, have in some cases created the wrong incentives. Some benefit owners have found themselves in a situation where they could be assigned more projects or resources than optimal for the organisation if they deliver overly optimistic business cases. By establishing systematic follow-up on benefits and costs for both technology and change, we ensure that the benefit owner's incentives are more in line with what is best for the organisation. Thus, by following up on benefits realisation and providing an overview of change and technology costs, we incentivise the benefit owners to provide cost and benefit estimates of higher quality for use in the ongoing prioritisation of projects.

Capacity Management

Capacity management is a key discipline in maximising the portfolio's benefits realisation. It clarifies the need for prioritisation by visualising the difference between the organisation's capacity and the demand for projects.

This transparency requires an estimation of resource needs in the projects and a decision on what capacity the organisation wishes to make available for projects. Suppose the organisation chooses not to let the PMO perform the capacity management task. In that case, it often results in the organisation having a portfolio of too many and overly long projects. Without capacity management, it is impossible to effectively link the projects' resource needs and the development capacity. In most cases, this means that it takes longer before the benefits are realised. At the same time, resource efficiency will often decrease because employees either work on too many different projects simultaneously (Søndergaard 2015) or because a lack of key resources in the projects makes it difficult for the rest of the project team to be effective.

Capacity to Handle Change

When the implementation of projects in many organisations has primarily been about producing technical deliverables, the PMO's task of capacity management has primarily been about calibrating the demand for technical development capacity with the organisation's capacity for producing technical deliverables. The benefit-driven PMO introduces three new capacity management services (cf. Figure 9.1). Two of these are related to establishing new behaviours. The first new service is managing capacity to create change. It includes the people who can take on the task as subproject managers and specialists in the projects' change track and the first-line managers and ambassadors who are part of the project. It is a service that typically resembles management of technical development capacity, simply with other employee groups.

Although we have the capacity to carry out both the technical track and change track in the project, it is not a foregone conclusion that the employees have the capacity to handle the change. Therefore, the second new change service consists of estimating the change capacity of the organisation's employees. A general business prioritisation is made of how many hours the organisation's employees must spend acquiring the new behaviour

Figure 9.2 Change capacity per employee group or department.

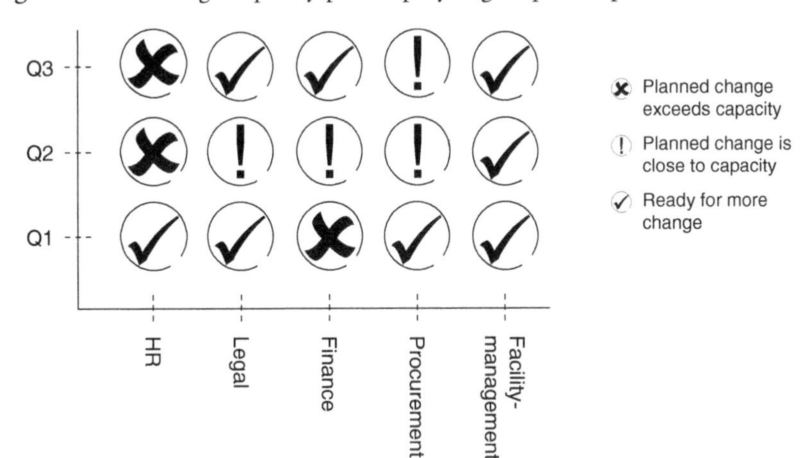

rather than solving current operational tasks. And at the same time, there is a more subjective assessment of how many changes the individual employee groups can handle.

When illustrating an employee group or department's capacity to handle change, it should be kept simple, owing to the subjective nature of the assessment. Figure 9.2 gives an example.

The figure shows the change capacity of different employee groups or departments three-quarters ahead with a simple red, yellow, or green indicator (indicated with a tick, exclamation mark and cross, respectively). Often, the managers of the individual departments or groups are the ones who assess what capacity is available. The assessment may be based on the following:

- Knowledge of the project pipeline in the organisation.
- An assessment of what the manager and ambassadors are expected to deliver for project participation.
- The time employees need to attain the desired behaviour.
- An assessment of the employees' ability to handle more changes in the coming quarters.

Capacity for Managing Benefits in Projects

The third new service includes managing the capacity to perform the tasks in the projects' benefit track. It involves ensuring that the projects are staffed to deliver on the benefits realisation tasks to be completed in the coming period. This service is similar to managing the capacity for the technical track, i.e. the part of the capacity that involves facilitating workshops, structuring the task of breaking down benefits, or advising in connection with the choice of estimation methods. That task typically lies with project managers or benefit specialists. The remaining capacity lies with the people in the business who are able to provide the professional input needed to make or update benefit estimates.

Performance Management

After the two service categories, portfolio management and governance as well as capacity management, it is time to look at the third category, namely performance management.

It includes setting and following up on goals for individual projects, just as performance management often includes goals for the overall portfolio. These could be efficiency goals, such as the number of completed projects per quarter or the average time for completing a project. It can also be strategic goals or goals for value creation, such as realised benefits for projects completed within the past 12 months.

For the technically driven PMOs, the primary task is to follow up on the projects' production of the technical deliverables, including the project triangle's[1] time, deliverables, and resources,

[1]The project triangle consists of three parts: resources, deliverables, and time. It describes the contract between the steering committee and the project manager, in which the project manager undertakes to deliver specific deliverables at an agreed time in exchange for an agreed budget to do so (Olsson et al. 2019).

as well as the project's risk level. When we start to place the same emphasis on change and benefits realisation as we do on the production of technical deliverables, we also introduce the need for more services in the performance management category. In the analysis phase, the projects have chosen a method for progress reporting on behavioural change.[2] Thus, the PMO gets the same type of overview on the progress of behavioural change as for the progress of the production of the technical deliverables. The benefits realisation method also introduces follow-up on benefits and the task of ensuring that the benefits we realise in the projects are also reflected in the organisation's budgets.

Aim for a Simple Data Collection

Benefit data is interesting for both the PMO and those who work with the organisation's budgets in the finance department. But the actual collection of benefit data is usually best placed in the PMO. The format of the collection is the project's benefits realisation plans (see Part 2) and should be collected by the PMO, which already handles all project data, in close collaboration with the projects and the benefit owners, who understand the projects' expected benefits. As with everything else, it is essential to keep data collection as simple as possible. That said, it is often necessary to have a dialogue with the benefit owners along the way about the individual projects and a complete list of projects for which they are responsible. The process of collecting benefit data often looks as illustrated in Figure 9.3.

The PMO initiates data collection every three months, for example. The PMO always communicates directly with the benefit owner, who then often delegates the actual data collection

[2] Methods for measuring progress in Part 3 include: behavioural data provided by IT systems, questionnaire surveys, interviews, and behavioural observations.

Figure 9.3 Collecting benefit data.

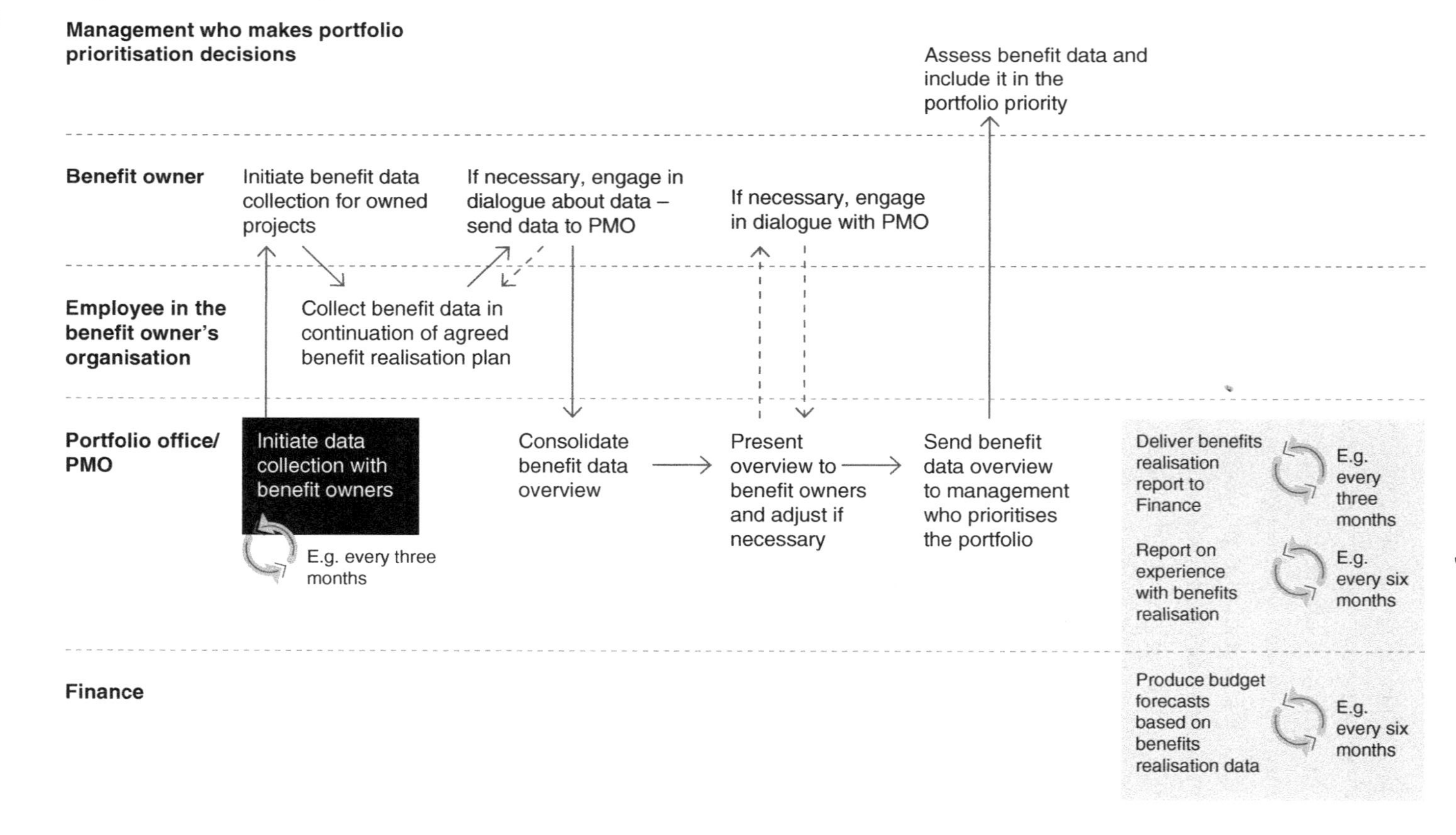

task to employees in the organisation. The PMO consolidates all benefits realisation data to make it easy to use the content as input for management's prioritisation of the portfolio. Before the consolidated overview is distributed, a dialogue takes place with the benefit owners who are not delivering the desired benefits. In this way, they get the opportunity to explain any deviation and possibly do some stakeholder management before the overview is distributed to the entire group of managers, who prioritise the portfolio.

Keep Budgets Up to Date

Finally, there is the task of ensuring that the organisation's budgets are updated as the benefits of the projects are realised. In most organisations, the finance department keeps track of the budgets, and both project costs and the majority of benefits from our projects should be reflected in the budgets. Benefits can either have a direct connection to budgets through increased revenue or reduced cost or an indirect connection because optimisations are converted into increased output (and revenue) instead of cost reductions. In organisations that work in a structured way with benefits realisation and change, the benefits realisation plan indicates when it is time to update the budgets. Here, it has been taken into account that the change must be in place before the benefits realisation occurs. Furthermore, changes in the project will be reflected on an ongoing basis in updates of the benefits realisation plan.

In practice, the finance department can update budgets and forecasts when the process of collecting benefit data has been completed, which is typically once every quarter (cf. Figure 9.3). If the benefits realisation plan contains benefits in the form of a reduction in the number of employees, it should take into account that the termination does not take place until we are confident that the desired change in behaviour is attained. This means that it takes a while before the behavioural change translates into financial savings in the budgets.

Before the organisation reaches a point where it works in a structured way with benefits realisation and change in all its projects, the question of when to update the budgets is important, especially when the answer has consequences for when the organisation reduces the number of employees. If the number of employees is reduced too soon, fewer employees have to handle the same number of tasks while acquiring new knowledge and behaviour, which in itself can take up a lot of time. The result may be an increased number of overtime hours, loss of productivity, postponement of the realisation of benefits, or cancellation of the change project and re-employment of employees.[3] Therefore, the interconnection of a project's benefits realisation to the finance department's budgets is often one of the last steps on the maturity ladder for the benefits realisation method, because without credible benefits realisation plans showing when benefits occur it is not practically possible.

Best Practice Support

The last category of services is best practice support. In some organisations, the framework for these services is also called a competency centre, and it can be an independent unit or part of the PMO.

[3]The Danish integrated e-health platform (Sundhedsplatformen) is an example that the new behaviour was not in place at the time of the planned start of benefit realisation, which meant extra overtime and a delay in the realisation of the desired benefits in the form of cost reductions in two years. Extract from Rigsrevisionen's report on Sundhedsplatformen submitted to the Public Accounts Committee. https://uk.rigsrevisionen.dk/Media/7/7/17-2017.pdf. The full Danish version can be found at: https://www.rigsrevisionen.dk/media/2104845/sr1717.pdf

The purpose of providing best practice support is to ensure consistent, high-quality project work across the portfolio. This is both for the benefit of the individual projects and an assurance that the data we use as a basis for prioritisation and capacity management has a comparably high quality. The first service under best practice support covers the need for support not directly linked to the project work in the analysis and execution phases. It includes support for innovation and idea development, start-up of large projects and programmes, and scrutiny and review – systematically at one or more times during the project's lifecycle or as needed. The three subsequent services are to ensure the quality of the work in each of the projects' three tracks: technical, change, and benefit.

Best practice support thus contributes to creating a high quality of work by ensuring the continual accumulation of experience and further development of the methods, processes, and tools used in the projects, including ongoing competency building and development of new behaviour among project managers, project participants, and benefit owners. Finally, the support entails assisting the projects, in the form of the ongoing implementation of improved best practices as well as executing specific tasks in one or more of the project's three tracks.

Development of a Benefit Catalogue

The technically driven PMO has a natural focus on the tasks in the technical track and the methods, processes, and tools that this part of the project work requires. The benefit-driven PMO also takes ownership and provides support for the use of the methods, processes, and tools that belong to the change track and the benefit track, which often includes the content from Parts 2 and 3 of this book. The knowledge we acquire across projects in the benefit track should be gathered into another tool, namely the benefit catalogue. Once the first projects have made benefit maps and benefits realisation plans, and the PMO has established a systematic follow-up procedure on benefits realisation as part of performance management, it makes sense to develop an actual benefit catalogue. The catalogue is a structured presentation of the organisation's experience with benefits realisation in projects.

In a benefit catalogue, the projects are typically divided according to the types of purposes we reviewed in Part 2, i.e. revenue, costs, compliance, and stakeholder satisfaction. If a project has more than one type of purpose, it can appear in several places in the catalogue.

A benefit catalogue usually contains:

- Typical end benefits, including the cause-effect chain: 'Behaviour-performance benefits-end benefits'.
- Examples of:
  - Benefit maps;
  - Benefits realisation plans;
  - Contacts for each example.
- Concrete experience data:
  - Benefit estimates (both performance benefits and end benefits) made in the analysis compared to realised benefits;
  - Explanations for deviation.

Benefit catalogues make many things easier. First, many projects are similar, so once you have completed a process optimisation project or a product launch project, there is typically much to be inspired by when you are preparing for the first benefits realisation workshop for future process optimisation or product launch projects. Further, it is often valuable to see how many benefits were realised, including how much of an effect similar projects had on the budgets. It can also help in the dialogue with the benefit owners so that previous experience can help set more realistic targets for the desired benefits.

The benefit catalogue does not have to be extensive to create value. The first good example of a benefit map or a benefits realisation plan creates value, even if there are no realised benefits yet. The first example often serves as proof that the method works, while the subsequent projects and benefit data collected from them contribute to more realistic estimates and improved project designs. In Part 5, I will use Ørsted as a case example of how to implement the benefits realisation method. Here you will also find an extract of Ørsted's benefit catalogue.

Appoint the Organisation's Method Specialists

The best practice support provided by the PMO requires that we identify the people in the organisation who can both own the method and have set aside time to help those projects that need support. There are many ways to approach method ownership, competency building, and support for project managers, project participants, and benefit owners. A solution where some of the organisation's project managers work as method specialists for one or more of the three project tracks has several advantages. First, it provides an opportunity to distribute knowledge and responsibility to more people. Second, it is beneficial for method development that the method specialist has fresh project experience to draw on. Finally, it is a cost-effective and flexible structure, where method development, competency building, help to change project behaviour, and delivery of internal consulting services can typically be adapted to the intensity of the projects the method specialist leads as the primary part of their job.

The use of method specialists has also proven to be a very effective method for implementing new methods, processes, and tools, including, for example, benefits realisation, if it does not exist as a subject matter area. It ensures ownership of the method and the local adaptation to the organisation's future development. Furthermore, it makes visible where you as a project manager, participant, or benefit owner can get help.

The Good Questions

In many organisations, the PMO is key to scaling benefits realisation to the entire organisation. So, if you have tried to work with the benefits realisation method without getting the full effect for the entire portfolio, ask yourself the following questions:

- 'Do we give our leaders the basis for decision-making they need to make decisions that maximise benefits realisation?'
- 'Do we give our project managers and benefit owners the support they need?'
- 'Do we use the PMO to create managerial demand for benefits realisation in the projects?'

In many cases, the answer to at least one of the questions is 'no'. In those cases, increasing the PMO's contribution to establishing a structured approach to benefits realisation and change throughout the organisation is often beneficial. The last part of the book focuses on unfolding the implementation of the benefits realisation method. That transformation may look different from organisation to organisation, but still the most successful organisations have several similarities. Ørsted is an excellent example of how implementing the benefits realisation method can take place in practice. Therefore, it is an excellent source of inspiration for how you and your organisation can take the next steps towards creating more value with your projects.

Part V

Implementing Benefits Realisation

10

Implementing Benefits Realisation

The ambition of the final part of the book is to provide inspiration for how to implement and anchor the benefits realisation method in your organisation. This will ensure that your change projects' benefit potential will be realised.

> *"Benefits realisation has helped Ørsted create significantly more value with our projects and epics[1] through better prioritisation decisions, clear managerial ownership, and structured follow-up."*
>
> Kenneth Theilgaard Roslind,
> Chief Digital Officer at Ørsted[2]

Throughout the book, we have dealt with how the benefits realisation method helps to increase value creation in projects. One of the most important conclusions has been that successful implementation of benefits realisation is very much about changing behaviour and that you can come a long way with just a few simple tools. At the same time, efficiently scaling the use of the

[1] Epics are described in Box 7.4: SAFe in brief.

[2] In the summer of 2021, Kenneth Theilgaard Roslind moved on within Ørsted to become Head of Business Applications and IT People Leadership in Kuala Lumpur.

benefits realisation method can be achieved with the help of a portfolio management office (PMO).

In this book, we have presented two cases: Nykredit (see Chapters 3–5) was driven by a desire to increase revenue through sales of new services and products. The University of Copenhagen (see Chapter 6) was motivated by an objective to find more efficient ways of working and increasing quality and the satisfaction of internal stakeholders. Implementing the benefits realisation method in your organisation is similar to the two cases as the value of using the method only materialises when there is a change in behaviour.

Implementing the Benefits Realisation Method Is a Change Project

All organisations are different, which means that there is more than one road to successfully implementing the benefits realisation method. Nevertheless, there are several important lessons to be learnt from the organisations that have benefitted the most from using the method. These lessons are in combined into a best practice plan for implementing the benefits realisation method in Figure 10.1. Since implementing the method is a change project, we should start the project by following the recommendations of Part 2. We should make a benefit map for the project, estimate the benefits, do the change analyses for the most critical employee groups, and analyse the technical deliverables.

Many of the technical deliverables (templates, scripts, and reporting formats) can be copied directly from this book. Therefore, the technical part of the analysis can be quite small. In many cases, it becomes an initial assessment of the need for local adaptation of the methods to fit into some of the current ways of working with projects. The part of the analysis that deals

Figure 10.1 Best practice plan for implementing the benefits realisation method.

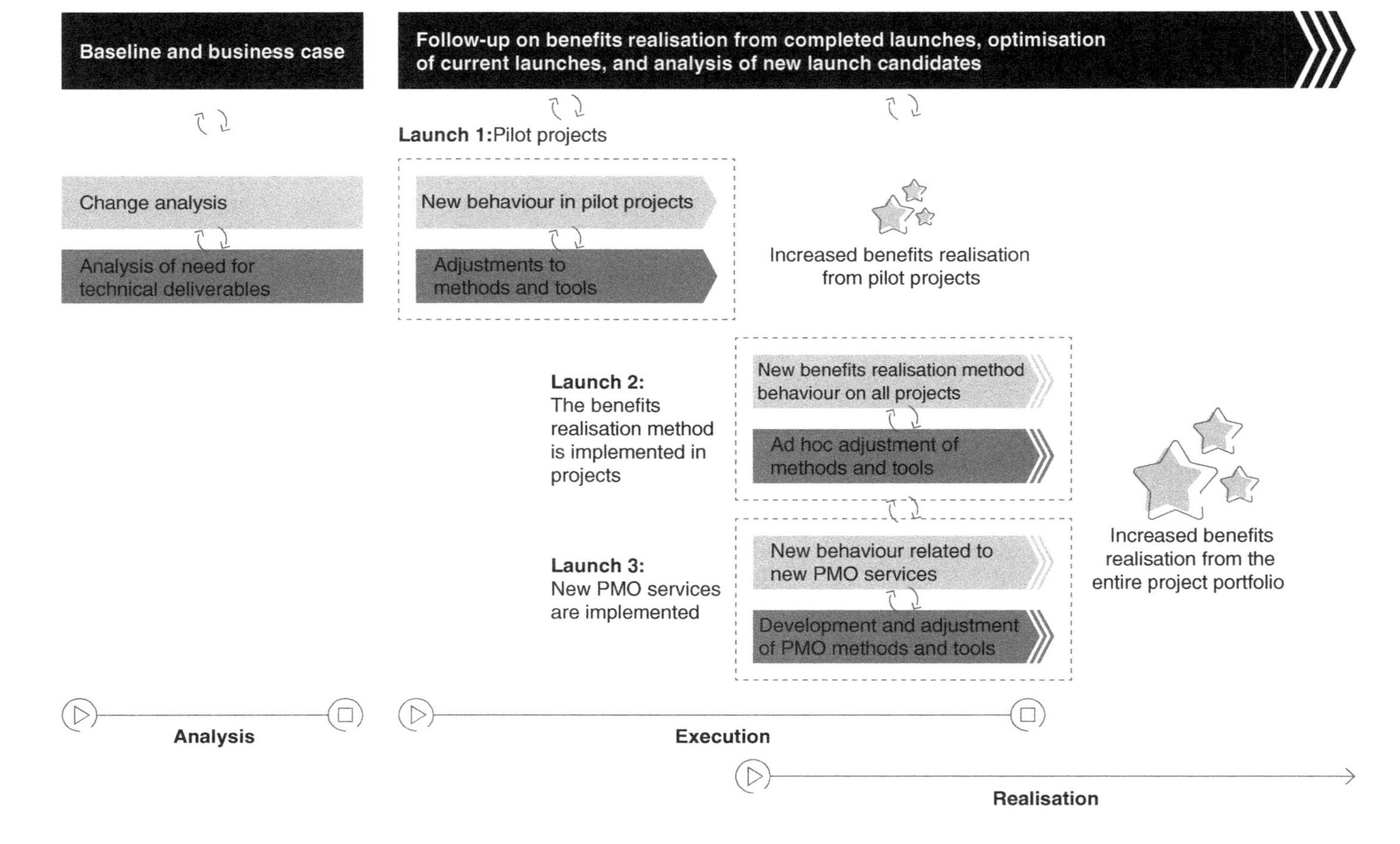

with establishing new services for the PMO may include an assessment of the services to be provided by the new PMO and the order in which they are to be launched. The PMO part may also contain a technical element in the form of new or upgraded tools for portfolio, capacity, and performance management. Still, the primary effort is usually in the benefit track and change track during the analysis phase.

Using Pilot Projects to Kick Off the Implementation

Once a business case has been prepared and approved for the project 'Implementing benefits realisation', the first launch in the execution phase is usually a test of the method in the form of two to six pilot projects, partly to test and update the assumptions from the analysis and partly, more importantly, to create success stories and ambassadors we can use when implementing the method to the rest of the projects in the portfolio. Launches 2 and 3 include implementing the benefits realisation method throughout the portfolio of change projects and, in parallel, establishing new portfolio management office (PMO) services, depending on the organisation's needs. In large organisations, launches 2 and 3 are often broken down into a series of launches. Usually, it is impossible to cover all projects at once as part of launch 2. The use of the method will most probably be spread to another 5–10 projects each quarter, depending on the support bandwidth of the method specialists. Apart from supporting projects, the method specialists might also train new method specialists as part of building the new best practice services in the PMO in launch 3.

Ørsted is one of the organisations that has created significantly more value using the benefits realisation method. In Chapter 11, Ørsted is used as an example of a successful implementation of the benefits realisation method when best practice meets reality in a large project organisation.

11

Implementing Benefits Realisation at Ørsted

Every year, Ørsted spends millions on business and product development with a focus on optimising and improving the company.

Ørsted is the world's most sustainable energy company and a world leader in developing offshore wind farms. The company employs approximately 6500 employees, 50 of whom are internal project managers or SAFe (scaled agile framework) scrum masters. Chief Digital Officer Kenneth Theilgaard Roslind was a key driver in Ørsted's change efforts. A few years back, he saw several examples of benefits not being realised. He therefore gathered a small project team to investigate whether a new approach to benefits realisation could increase the value creation in their projects.

The team's establishment became the starting point for a project called 'Benefits Management'. The project not only helped to realise far more benefits in Ørsted's projects and epics but also introduced a shared language and awareness of benefits realisation and value creation. This became a lever for Ørsted's

Figure 11.1 Phases in Ørsted's 'Benefits Management' project.

ambition to make its digitisation efforts even more value focused. The project was carried out in three main phases, as shown in Figure 11.1.[1]

The analysis and concept development phase included benefit track and change track activities from Part 2 of the book, including developing a benefit map and an analysis of the size of the behavioural change. The phase also included a technical track, which analysed the need for new templates and tools and the development of a concept for realising benefits with minimum viable product (MVP) versions[2] of key templates, scripts, and tools. After the analysis and concept development phase was completed, the business case was approved, and the project went directly to the second phase: pilot projects.

The pilots were a proof-of-concept test for whether the method could work at Ørsted and a way to gather knowledge on what it would take to ensure effective implementation. The last phase, 'Implementation', focused on the behavioural change itself. The primary approach was to train a number of internal consultants to become method specialists and let them drive the change and implementation at Ørsted, including supporting

---

[1] Ørsted's phase plan is very similar to the best practice plan in Figure 10.1. The execution phase at Ørsted is divided into a "Pilot projects" phase and an "Implementation" phase. The content of the "Pilot projects" at Ørsted is similar to launch 1, and "Implementation" includes launches 2 and 3 of the best practice plan.

[2] MVP versions of templates, scripts, and tools meant that the company had materials of sufficiently good quality to be used in the pilot projects, but that they had to be further developed based on the knowledge Ørsted gained while executing the pilot projects.

both managers and employees in working with benefits realisation and further developing the method. In the following sections, we dive into the three main phases of Ørsted's implementation of the benefits realisation method.

Phase 1: Analysis and Concept Development

Kenneth Theilgaard Roslind chose to have a taste of his own medicine and use the benefits realisation method on the 'Benefits Management' project.

Thus, the analysis phase was not simply about adapting the benefits realisation method to fit Ørsted's project management language. It was also about developing a benefit map and doing the work within the benefit track and change track. Therefore, the analysis phase of Ørsted's 'Benefits Management' project consisted of activities spread over the three tracks we would usually use in benefit-driven change projects:

- Baseline for benefits realisation, benefit map, and estimation of the benefit potential (benefit track).
- Analysis of the change for managers and project managers (the change track).
- Concept description for the use of benefits realisation at the project and portfolio level (technical track).

The baseline for benefits realisation at Ørsted was similar to the one most organisations have if they have not previously worked with benefits realisation in a structured manner. Business cases with benefit estimates had been prepared for most projects. Still, no process across Ørsted ensured a general and systematic follow-up of the realised benefits after the projects had been initiated. Therefore, there was no data across Ørsted showing which benefits the projects realised, just as it was not documented who owned the benefits. Therefore, the baseline work concluded, 'There is a great demand for introducing a standardised approach to benefits realisation' (Figure 11.2).

Developing a Benefit Map

The benefit map that Ørsted developed for 'Benefits Management' is shown in Figure 11.3. It is an excellent example of what a benefit map typically looks like. The benefit map was initially created with coloured index cards together with one of Ørsted's IT boards responsible for the overall strategic prioritisation of projects and epics in a business unit. The map was then further matured in the benefit track until it appeared as shown in the figure at the end of the analysis phase.

Ørsted's benefit map shows that the implementation of 'Benefits Management' has three purposes:

- Get a larger ROI (return on investment) from projects.
- Realise the same benefits with a reduced scope, called 'scope efficiency'.
- Enable strategic portfolio management by using credible benefit and cost data from projects.

Like many other organisations, Ørsted had challenges in quantifying the value of implementing the benefits realisation method. In a typical change project, we compare the As-Is situation with the To-Be situation: what value are we creating now and what value creation will we get in the future when the change is implemented? The difference is the benefit generated by the project. In an implementation of the benefits realisation method, it is difficult to make that comparison. Partly because, we often lack data on the current benefits realisation. Partly because, we

Figure 11.2 Ørsted's baseline for benefits realisation.

The established baseline indicates that there is a great need to introduce a standardised approach to benefits realisation

BUSINESS CASE OBSERVATIONS*

19% Have identified benefits for both IT and business

26% Have not identified benefits

Benefit owners are not appointed

There is no guide to follow up on benefits

DATA

- Information and overview of current and past projects are not easily accessible.
- Business cases are insufficient and too different to be easily compared.
- Quality varies, making it difficult to assess actual realised benefits.

PRIORITISATION

- Varying business case content makes it difficult to prioritise projects.
- Lack of actual benefits realisation from projects can lead to wrong decisions.
- Prioritising projects based on expected future benefits is difficult.

MANAGEMENT

- There is no evidence that projects are led to maximise benefits realisation or to minimise costs.
- There is no culture in place to define benefits or define the need for new behaviour.
- There is no clear governance on how to follow up on benefits after projects are completed.

*Based on 31 projects from one of Ørsted's business units.

Figure 11.3 Ørsted's benefit map for implementation of 'Benefits Management'.

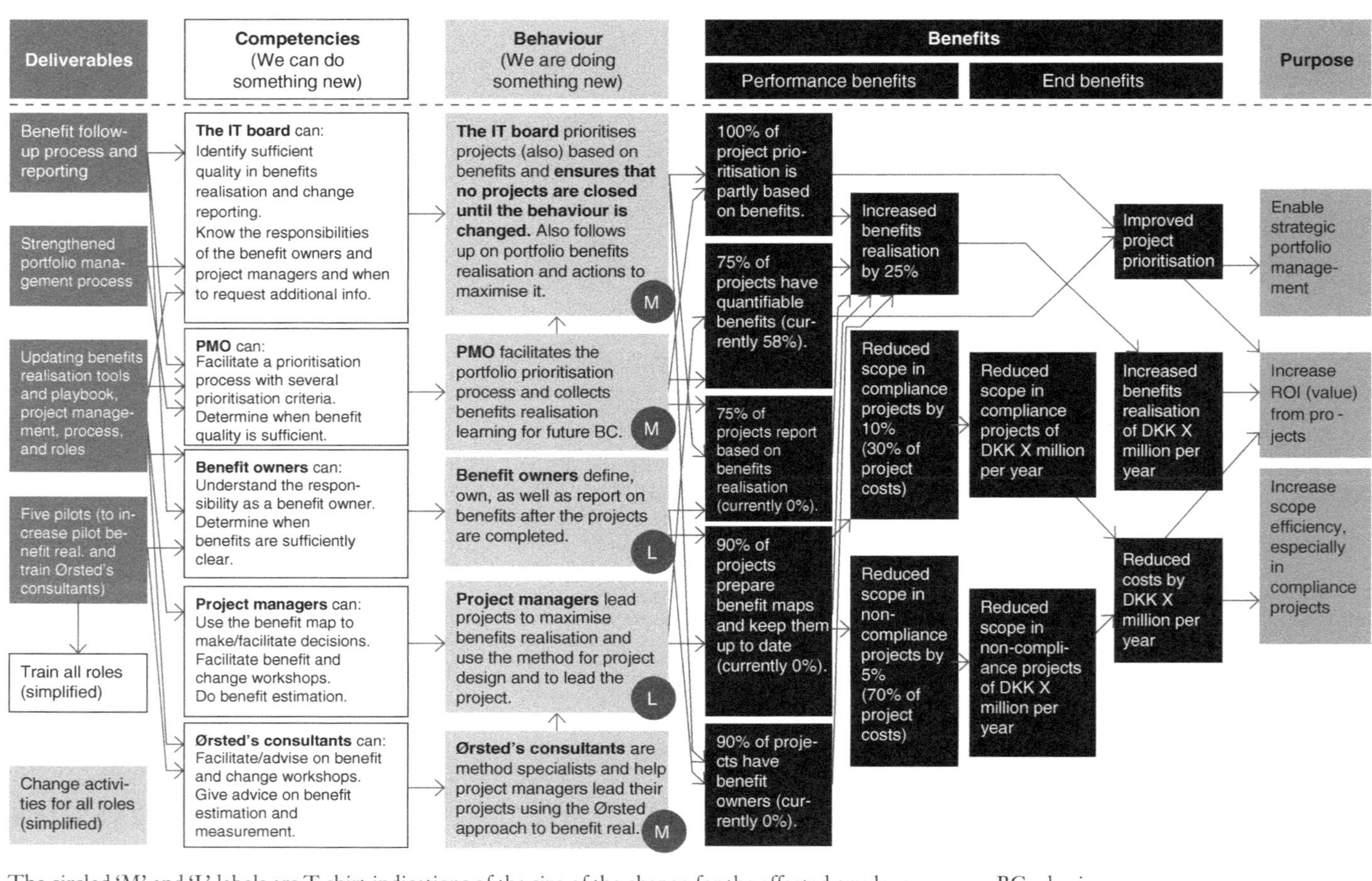

The circled 'M' and 'L' labels are T-shirt indications of the size of the change for the affected employee groups. BC – business case.

cannot compare the benefits from the current project portfolio with the benefits from a future project portfolio as the projects, and thus the benefits realisation in the two portfolios, will be different.[3]

Conservative Assessment of the Benefits

When implementing the benefits realisation method, the measurable and traceable benefits are often the improvements in performance that are the immediate result of changed behaviour. For example, 'Ninety per cent of all projects have a benefit owner' or 'Seventy-five per cent of all projects report on benefits realisation.'

To get an idea of the size of the financial benefits that were expected to be realised, Ørsted made a conservative estimate. The estimate was based on already documented benefits and calculated as an added percentage of that figure. Furthermore, a similar type of calculation was made to get an idea of how large a cost-saving could be achieved by having the right (reduced) scope on the projects. Finally, estimates were also made of the cost of producing the technical deliverables, building competencies, and changing behaviour, which was the costliest part of the project. For Ørsted, the business case looked positive, so they decided to implement the benefits realisation method through the project 'Benefits Management'.

---

[3] In order to make an academic, correct documentation of the effect of benefit realisation, you can assess the benefit realisation for a project where the benefit realisation method has been used and compare it with three comparable reference projects where the method has not been used. It provides better data to assess the method, but it is also a more costly method and therefore often difficult to use in practice. Inspired by Rode et al. (2021).

Experience Gained from the Analysis and Concept Development Phase

The project's first phase showed great potential to continue working with the benefits realisation method. At the end of the phase, it was difficult to predict how important the work in the analysis phase would prove to be in the subsequent part of the project. Ørsted's decision to make both a baseline and a benefit map was essential for the design of the project. At the same time, it was a very important tool when communicating with stakeholders at all levels of the organisation throughout the project. Ørsted's baseline was important when discussing the potential and provided a basis for documenting and celebrating the progress made along the way. The benefit map served as an example of what a benefit map looks like and visualised the benefits and the change on which the project depended. Finally, the benefit map showed that the project team believed in their own concept and thus invested time in making the project's baseline and benefit map.

Phase 2: Pilot Projects

After the analysis was completed and the 'Benefits Management' project had been approved, Ørsted tested the assumptions behind the benefit map: the actual benefits, the feasibility of the project, and the costs of changing behaviour in five pilot projects.

The work also included validation of the analysis's assumptions about the status of the project and whether the expectations of the managers and project managers' reactions to the introduction of benefits realisation were true. The pilot projects served as a field study and a series of pilot implementations.[4] The pilot projects also provided an opportunity to strengthen the later

[4] Figure 5.3: Methods for estimating benefits and Box 8.1: Field studies.

implementation, as they started building the competencies of the pilots' project managers, steering committee members, and internal consultants. Most importantly, the pilots helped to create positive stories about the value of using the benefits realisation method in the organisation.

If Ørsted were to measure the full extent of the value of the benefits realisation method, based on actual ROI and benefits realisation, it would take several years. Therefore, Ørsted chose a different approach. The project team assessed the potential of the benefits realisation method by reviewing the pilot projects' benefit maps and benefits realisation plans. Then they discussed what the benefits realisation method had meant for the choice of deliverables, change of behaviour, and the identified benefits compared to similar projects.

The test of assumptions behind the benefit map on the pilot projects confirmed the benefit potential. Ørsted would gain a much higher benefits realisation from the substantial investment in both projects and epics, while scope could be significantly reduced in many projects and epics. The conclusion was that Ørsted should gradually implement the benefits realisation method throughout the organisation.

Experience from the Pilot Projects

After the analysis in the first phase showed a need to work in a structured way with the benefits realisation method, the pilots in the second phase confirmed that benefits realisation was the right method for Ørsted. The pilots were crucial to the legitimacy that the benefits realisation method gained in the organisation. To the rest of the organisation, Ørsted could now document that benefits realisation would create value. At the same time, Ørsted had a much better knowledge of what a full implementation of the benefits realisation method would require. On a practical level, the pilot projects worked well as an opportunity to test and adapt Ørsted's benefits realisation concept, including templates, scripts, and tools. The pilot projects proved to be an excellent opportunity to get off to a flying start in the subsequent 'Implementation' phase. Partly by using them to start building the competencies of involved project managers, steering committee members, and internal consultants (method specialists), and partly to adapt the approach to implementing benefits realisation based on the newly gained experience.

The pilots also clarified that Ørsted could have gained even greater value if more time and effort had been invested in mobilising the pilot projects' steering committees and the internal consultants. Some managers saw benefits realisation as an additional task and a responsibility they had not asked for or had any influence on. Thus, the change task in the pilots became greater and meant that a few managers did not get the ownership that others had. That experience was invaluable when planning the subsequent implementation. Another discovery was that a lengthy mobilisation of Ørsted's internal consultants meant they only participated in two out of five pilot projects. The project group behind 'Benefits Management' conducted three pilot projects alone. As a result, the internal consultants missed part of the training. In retrospect, it meant that including these employees now had to be done as extra work during the implementation phase.

Phase 3: Implementing New Behaviour at Ørsted

The project's first two phases were to prepare and clarify how to succeed with benefits realisation at Ørsted. The aim of the implementation phase was to change the way of working with projects and epics in general.

'Implementing the benefits realisation method is a change project where we need to get senior management, managers in the steering committees, and employees on board to succeed.'

Kenneth Theilgaard Roslind,
Chief Digital Officer at Ørsted

Now was the time to establish the new behaviour. The project team knew that implementing the benefits realisation method would affect most of the digital content development in the company and thus also a lot of people. The key to success was to change the behaviour of two key employee groups: the managers in the steering committees and the project managers. In the project, it was illustrated as shown in Figure 11.4.

The experience from the implementation showed that, even though the project managers and Ørsted's consultants (method specialists) are facing the largest practical change, the new method also requires a change in the behaviour of the managers.

Figure 11.4 'The pincer': success requires a change for managers in the steering committees as well as for project managers.

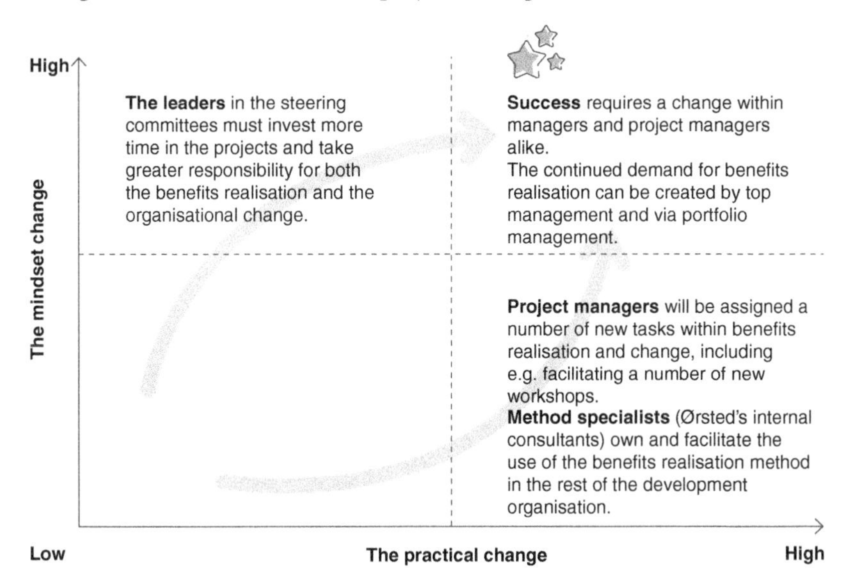

They have to insist that the benefits realisation method is used, and own the benefits and the change needed to realise those benefits. The new behaviour of managers does not require new practical competencies. It requires a new mindset – a commitment to creating and tracking results at the project level instead of the department or division level they are used to.

Ensuring Future Ownership

The first step in phase 3 was to place the future ownership of the benefits realisation method. The ownership was placed with a group of internal consultants who were to become the future method specialists in benefits realisation and change.

To succeed with the change, Ørsted made an implementation plan consisting of three launches, shown in Figure 11.5.

The first launch consisted of anchoring the benefits realisation method among Ørsted's internal consultants. Launch 2 was to ensure the implementation of the benefits realisation method in all projects. As it was impossible to implement the benefits realisation method in all projects simultaneously, projects in the initial stages were given priority. In contrast, projects that were

Figure 11.5 The three launches in Ørsted phase 3: 'implementation'.

Launch of implementation of benefits realisation at Ørsted

Launch 1: Anchoring the benefits realisation method among internal consultants

Launch 2: Implementation of the benefits realisation method on all early-stage projects (scope modified to include the SAFe method during implementation)

Launch 3: Implementation of adjusted portfolio management in business units (scope modified to include the SAFe method during implementation)

planned to end soon were allowed to be completed without modification. Launch 3 included implementing adjusted portfolio management in individual business units as enough projects using the benefits realisation method came along. An overlap was planned between launches 1 and 2 and launches 2 and 3. Ørsted's internal consultants were to start advising colleagues on benefits realisation and change as soon as they were ready to take on the method specialist role. Launch 3 was to occur as individual business units had enough projects in their portfolio working with the benefits realisation method that would justify changing the portfolio management.

That was the original plan. But the reality of project work is that organisations are (fortunately) never static. While implementing the benefits realisation method, Ørsted decided to introduce the SAFe method, first as an addition to projects in part of the organisation, later as the primary method of producing deliverables.

Adaptions to SAFe

The SAFe method was intended to increase the efficiency of software development for Ørsted. For the 'Benefits Management' project, the introduction of SAFe meant several customisations during the implementation of the benefits realisation method. Launch 2, which implemented benefits realisation for all projects, was expanded to include both projects and SAFe. Launch 3, which implemented adjusted portfolio management, changed the scope so that portfolio management would operate to a considerable extent within the framework of SAFe.[5] Although it

[5] Read Box 7.4: SAFe in brief.

initially required several customisations in the third stage, the decision to merge benefits realisation into the SAFe framework made sense.

The following sections describe how the benefits realisation method was implemented for the main employee groups.

Anchoring the Benefits Realisation Method with Ørsted's Internal Consultants

A significant milestone in launch 1 was the dissolution of the internal project team that had started the 'Benefits Management' project. The dissolution was necessary to hand over full responsibility for completing the implementation to the internal consultants. At the same time, it passed on responsibility for the future ownership and support of the benefits realisation method (support for project managers, scrum masters, and managers in the steering committees) and the responsibility for further development of the method.

To transfer full responsibility for implementing the 'Benefits Management' project to the internal consultants, the project team needed to enable them to help the rest of the organisation. The efforts to create the desired behaviour among the internal consultants consisted of a combination of change deliverables, training deliverables, and technical deliverables, as illustrated in Figure 11.6. The technical deliverables were Ørsted's benefits realisation concept, updated with the experience from the pilot projects and later additions resulting from the introduction of the SAFe method. The training deliverables consisted of a training course followed by two rounds of follow-up focusing on feedback and coaching on the benefits realisation work the internal consultants had done on their projects. Finally, the change deliverable consisted of discussing and co-creating the design of how the internal consultants could help project managers and

Figure 11.6 Efforts to create new behaviour among internal consultants.

Deliverables	
Technical deliverables	**Benefits realisation concept** • New roles and responsibilities. • Linking the benefits realisation method to current development processes. • Templates, playbooks, and reporting formats. The concept was updated in phases 2 and 3 with experience from the pilot projects and the inclusion of SAFe.
Training deliverables	**Two-day course** Case-based training with focus on new roles and tools. **Two half-day follow-ups** Focus on the benefits realisation work on own projects, including feedback and inspiration from other Ørsted projects.
Change deliverables	**Design of new behaviour** Designing how the internal consultants should help project managers and benefit owners (also used for training). **On-the-job help and sparring** On-the-job help and sparring in connection with the use of the benefits realisation method on Ørsted's projects and epics.

managers in the steering committees combined with on-the-job support as needed.

The internal consultants had different starting points. Some had been involved in the pilot projects, others not, just as they had diverse backgrounds as internal consultants and facilitators. Different starting points combined with different opportunities to free up time to get on-the-job support and training meant that the training of the internal consultants was completed on an ongoing basis.

The Change in Behaviour for Project Managers

As the internal consultants received training and were given the possibility to free up time, they were now able to take on the role of method specialists and carry out the task of helping project managers. The efforts to help them change their behaviour focused on three things:

- To reduce competency barriers and establish a shared language through training to reduce the demand for support from internal consultants.
- To make the use of the benefits realisation method as easy as possible, increasing the chance of success, and reduce the demand for support from internal consultants.
- To make it easy and acceptable to get support from internal consultants to ensure high-quality work in the benefits realisation and change tracks.

The internal consultants developed a training course for the 60 project managers, scrum masters, and product owners called BAT (benefit academy training). During the training, the participants acquired new competencies, and it was clarified how the internal consultants could help them in the change process when needed.

Scripts and materials were made readily accessible to make it easy. A benefit catalogue and an overview of benefits realisation examples on Ørsted projects were created, which could serve as inspiration or be reused with minor updates (see Box 11.1). The desired behaviour was exemplified in different situations. At steering committee meetings, one of the examples of new behaviour was that the project managers used the benefit map to discuss project status, risks, and new opportunities. Using the benefit map as a reference point for these discussions made it easy to put the consequences into perspective, such as the reduction in benefits caused by a deliverable the organisation is not able to produce.

Box 11.1 The benefit catalogue makes it easier to work with benefits realisation

To simplify describing benefits and improving the quality of the descriptions, Ørsted created a benefit catalogue with typical benefits, including negative ones. Figure 11.7 shows an overview of the end benefits.[6] Each end benefit has a definition and examples of how they can be quantified, including whether the benefit should be linked to budgets. Table 11.1 offers a description of each benefit.

Figure 11.7 Ørsted's overview of end benefits.

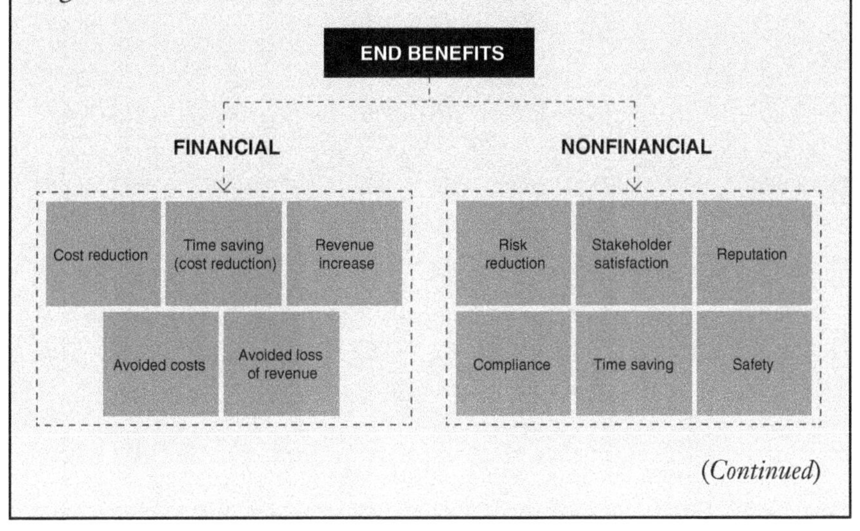

(Continued)

[6] End benefits are described in Chapter 4.

Table 11.1 Detailed description of each benefit. The financial benefits "Cost reduction" and "Time saving" are used as examples.

Category	Cost reduction	Time saving(thereby cost reduction)
Definition	When a specific cost is reduced as a consequence of a change. Can be an operating (OPEX) or capitalised (CAPEX) cost. The saving can be included in the budget	In order for a time saving to be a financial benefit in the form of a cost reduction, the cost of resources in a department must be reduced. The saving can be included in the budget.
Benefit example	• Reduced software license cost • Move tasks from A to B • Lower LCOE (Levelized Cost of Energy)	Reduced number of FTEs in X department.
Measurement/KPI	• Reduced cost of licenses in Euro per year • Reduced resource cost in Euro per year • LCOE reduced by X% per kWh	Reduced resource cost of X Euro per year in department X.
Can be included in the budget	Yes	Yes

Establishing Benefits Realisation Support for SAFe

The introduction of SAFe in Ørsted made it necessary to find a way to merge the benefits realisation method with the SAFe method. The SAFe method had to gain a foothold in Ørsted before Kenneth Theilgaard Roslind and the internal consultants could define how SAFe and benefits realisation should link up. The ambition for using the benefits realisation method and SAFe in both projects ended up being formulated like this:

> *We want to have an end-to-end focus on (and make) benefits management the common denominator regardless of project/epic status and choice of execution method.*

Ørsted chose a model in which the internal consultants were responsible for developing ideas and the first part of the work, which is typically done during the analysis phase. Thus, the internal consultants facilitated the first benefits realisation workshop, made an early estimation of benefits, and facilitated an early estimation of both the organisational change and the technical development. Only when Ørsted chooses to invest in a well-researched idea will it be decided whether the deliverables should be produced in the framework of a project or in SAFe. Regardless of the choice of delivery method, the internal consultants will take over again when technical development and organisational change have been completed to follow up on the benefits realisation. If help with benefits realisation or change is needed along the way, the project manager or scrum master can also get help from the internal consultants.

Figure 11.8 shows an example of an idea with initially three benefits that are identified and matured. Benefits and scope change along the way as there is greater knowledge about the possibilities for benefits realisation.

Figure 11.8 Common approach to benefits realisation regardless of delivery method.

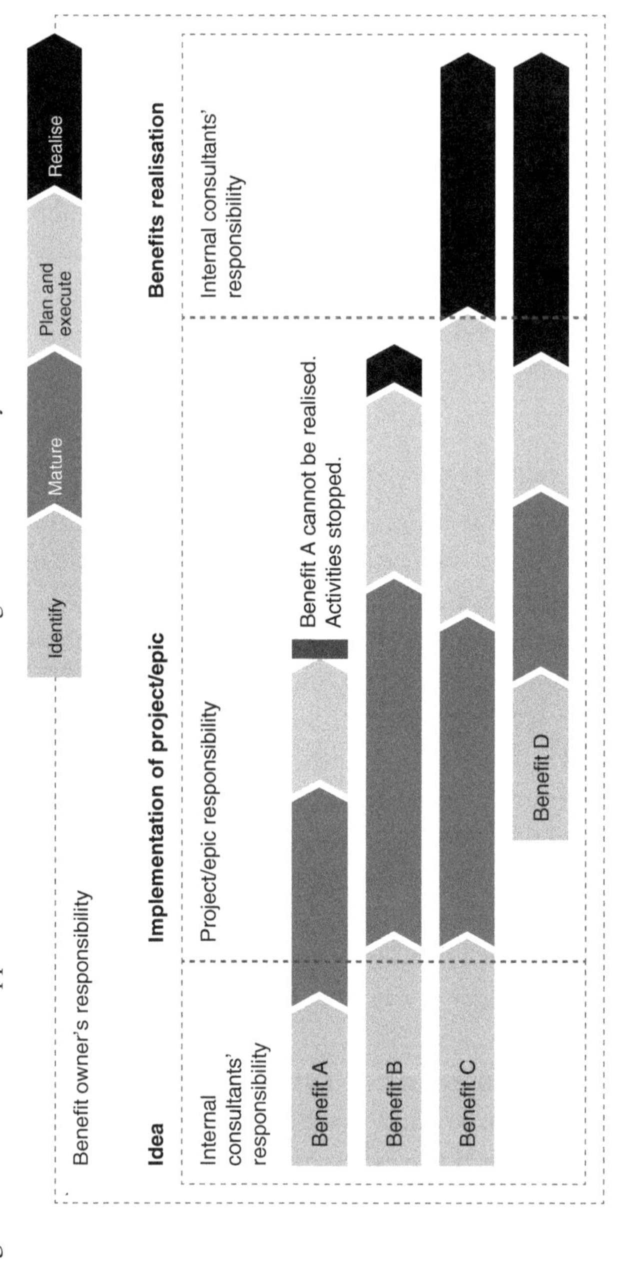

The names of the roles in the figure have been changed to match the naming of roles used in the book.

At portfolio level, Ørsted introduced a three-month prioritisation cadence that included development using both projects and the SAFe method, so projects and epics could be initiated, stopped, or completed at the same point in time. After they were prioritised, the projects proceeded with a benefit track, change track, and technical track as described in the benefit-driven change model in Chapter 2. Ørsted's SAFe setup is similar to the setup described in Chapter 7. The fact that Ørsted succeeded in creating a shared framework for the development of both projects and epics also meant that common goals could be formulated for implementing benefits realisation across delivery methods. With common goals, there was a basis for celebrating successes across delivery methods, for example when 100% of all new projects and epics had completed the first version of the benefit map and identified quantifiable benefits.

Changing the Behaviour of the Managers in the Steering Committees

Just as Carsten Kruse from Nykredit had to be persuaded to enter the first benefits realisation workshop, it also took an effort to get managerial support at Ørsted.[7] The managers most affected were those on the steering committees who were benefit owners and members of the division management teams at Ørsted. Of course, many saw an advantage in the fact that greater benefits realisation was both valuable for Ørsted and made it easier for them to achieve their goals, while at the same time being faced with greater demands concerning participation and responsibility in the projects.

Two things helped to change the managers' behaviour. First, Kenneth Theilgaard Roslind was an active sponsor who took the

[7] The case of Nykredit and Carsten Kruse's role as sponsor of benefit realisation is described in Chapters 3–5.

time to continually elaborate on the purpose and the value their involvement would create. That generated interest and demand for benefits realisation at the senior management level, which affected the managers in the layer below. In addition, senior management's involvement and demand for benefit estimates, updates, and tracking were systematically passed on through the adjusted portfolio management. Systematic demand from the portfolio level made benefits realisation mandatory, thus creating a level playing field for all. In this way, all managers who participated in steering committees assessed their development wishes on the same scale and were held accountable for benefits realisation in the same way.

Implementation advice from Ørsted

The third phase, the most comprehensive and resource-intensive in the project, contributed to the internal consultants, management, and Ørsted as an organisation becoming more knowledgeable about benefits realisation and change – and they began to reap the benefits from the 'Benefits Management' project.

With the lessons learnt from the implementation of benefits realisation, Kenneth Theilgaard Roslind has four pieces of advice for organisations that take on the task:

- **Implement the benefits realisation method step by step.** Use pilots to test the concept, build support, incorporate new learnings continually, and spread the use of the benefits realisation method incrementally to the individual parts of the organisation. This ensures that the internal consultants (method specialists) have the capacity to support the change.
- **Anchor the method among method specialists.** Benefits realisation and behavioural change are two disciplines that often require experience from several projects to become

good at it. Therefore, training method specialists who can own the method and support the rest of the organisation with training, coaching, and facilitation support offer an effective way to achieve benefits realisation and a structured approach for changing behaviour implemented.

- **Create demand for benefits realisation through senior management and portfolio management.** As in other change projects, anchoring with senior management is essential to the success of any broad implementation. Using portfolio management effectively to convey senior management's commitment is a significant lever for changing the behaviour of project managers and managers in the steering committees.
- **Make it easy to do the right thing.** It also works at Ørsted. Designing easy-to-facilitate workshops, tools such as the benefit catalogue, and formats for steering committee meetings helps create the desired behaviour. It makes it easier to apply the new behaviour and removes good reasons not to.

For Ørsted to maintain their position as the world leader in offshore wind farms, they continually optimise their development organisation. Thus, their approach to delivery production, benefits realisation, and behavioural change is constantly being optimised. New methods are being tested and implemented. Continual improvements in the approach to benefits realisation and change are anchored with the internal consultants. In this way, methods, employees, and managers are kept updated on the latest and best ways of working for Ørsted to realise as many benefits as possible.

12

Implementing the Benefits Realisation Method in Your Organisation

The best start to implementing the benefits realisation method is to remember that it does not simply happen by introducing a set of new tools.

It is mostly a change in behaviour for the managers in the steering committees and for project managers. It is a change in the way we see projects and our development efforts. And it is a change where we park some of our current ideas and practices.

Through the first three parts of the book, you have gained a practical and case-based guide on how you and your organisation can get more out of your change projects. This forms the core of a new way of looking at and working with projects to create the change that ensures you realise the potential benefits. The key points are summarised here:

- Benefits realisation is created in a process based on cause-and-effect relationships. If benefits, the need for new behaviour, competencies, or technical deliverables change along the way, it will have consequences for the rest of the project.

- Design the project the right way. Use the benefits realisation workshop to clarify how the project will create value and what change it requires.
- Change projects have three tracks: the benefit track, the change track, and the technical track. Benefits realisation results from the work and interaction between these three tracks throughout the duration of the project.
- Successful change requires a structured analysis effort in the same way that technical development does. Use the change workshop as the practical starting point for the change analysis.
- The benefits change during the project. Analyse, optimise, and follow up on benefits realisation continually and after the project is completed.
- See the change of behaviour as a process. Develop and test your approach to change with (some of) the people it is all about – the people who need to change their ways of working. Do it before you launch the change efforts for a large group of colleagues.
- Use behavioural design to create new ways of working that deliver benefits to both the organisation and the people who are changing behaviour.
- Make it as easy as possible. Go out and meet your colleagues, learn more about their everyday lives, and make it as easy and attractive as possible to change behaviour.

The PMO Plays a Key Role

The successful use of the benefits realisation method on a few projects is good. Still, if the entire organisation's benefit potential is to be redeemed, there is a need to implement the benefits realisation method throughout the organisation. The fourth part of the book discusses how the portfolio management office (PMO) can help get the benefits realisation method scaled to the rest of the organisation. The PMO's role in implementation is central in creating demand for benefits realisation estimates and follow-up and providing the necessary support for the project managers, change managers, and benefit owners who are embracing the new ways of working. The key points for implementing and further developing benefits realisation and maximising benefits realisation across the portfolio are summarised here:

- Consider the implementation of the benefits realisation method as a change project. Let yourself be inspired by Ørsted, go back to Parts 2 and 3 of this book and invest some time in the benefit track and change track needed in your organisation to transform the way you work with both.
- Pay special attention to the benefit owners, project managers, change managers, PMO managers, and the new method specialists. It is their new behaviour that is crucial to success.
- Use the PMO to create demand for benefits realisation and a structured approach to change. Require updated benefit maps, benefits realisation plans, change estimates, and change plans.
- Upgrade your technically driven PMO to a benefit-driven PMO. Benefits realisation and change must be part of the PMO's capacity management, performance management, and best practice support, ensuring that management can make the best possible decisions to develop the organisation.

And finally, find the manager in the organisation who will be the benefit owner and champion for implementing benefits realisation in your organisation and help them create successful changes.

As a final inspiration to you, who, after reading this book, believes your organisation could also profit from implementing benefits realisation and organisational change, please see the suggestions in Box 12.1 for which activities and best practices an implementation plan could contain.

From here, there is only one thing to say: enjoy!

Box 12.1 Implementing the benefits realisation method: suggestions for activities

The content of this box is intended to inspire you on how to approach the implementation of the benefits realisation method. The starting point is the best practice plan shown in Figure 10.1, which has been reimplemented in Figure 12.1.

Figure 12.1 Best practice plan for implementing benefits realisation.

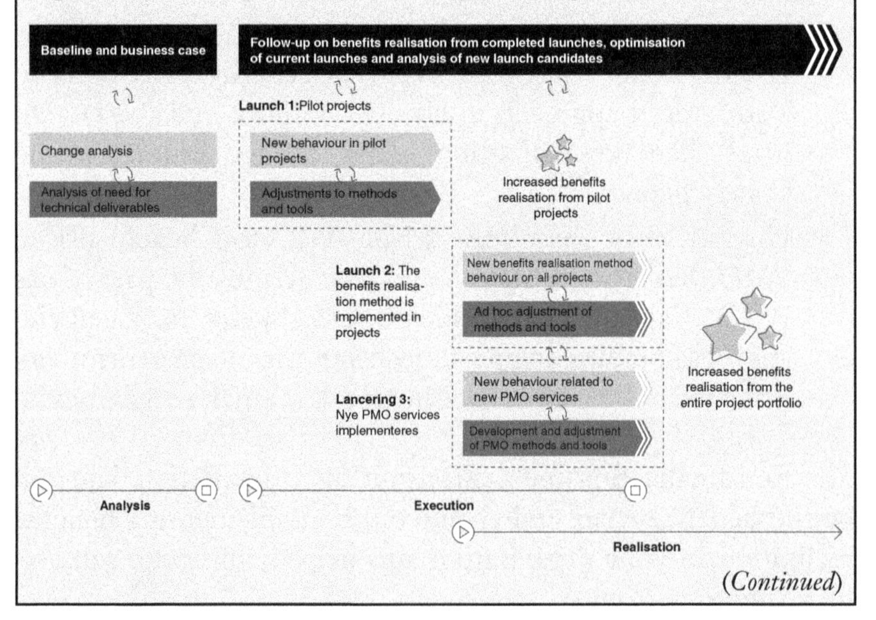

(Continued)

(*Continued*)

Recommended main activities in the analysis phase

The benefit track

- Prepare a simple baseline, for example as Ørsted's baseline in Figure 11.2.
- Prepare a benefit map, benefit estimates, and a benefits realisation plan.

The change track

- Prepare an analysis of the change for key stakeholders (often project managers, change managers, steering committee participants/benefit owners, method specialists, and PMO management).

The technical track

- Develop a benefits realisation concept consisting of a brief presentation with motivation and introduction to the method and the first version of templates and tools, for example from Parts 2 and 3 of this book. In addition, it may include an initial assessment of the need to customise templates and tools against the versions in this book.

Recommended main activities in the execution phase

The benefit track typically includes:

- Continual update of the benefit map and benefits realisation plan.

(*Continued*)

(Continued)

- Follow-up on benefits realisation, especially performance benefits such as 'Number of projects with quantifiable benefits'. See also Ørsted's benefit map in Figure 11.3.
- After the project is completed, follow-up on benefits becomes part of the updated performance management in the PMO.

Note: the benefit track is the same for launches 1, 2, and 3.

Launch 1: Pilot projects

Kick-off and initial training

- Participants are often the pilot project's benefit owners/steering committee, project managers, change managers, and method specialists (similar to Ørsted's internal consultants).

Pilot projects – two to six

- The pilot projects can be selected to represent the project types that are most commonly executed in the organisation.
- The pilot projects typically include:
  - Benefit track (benefit map, benefit estimation, benefits realisation plan, and ensuring ownership).
  - Change track (change analysis, possibly combined with a field study and parts of the effort to change behaviour).

(Continued)

(Continued)

Note: the pilot projects can be extended to include a technical track if the organisation also wants to test a more efficient approach to producing technical deliverables. Otherwise, we only interact with the people working in the technical track without interfering with how the work is done.

Updating the business case and concept for benefits realisation

- Updating the benefits and the implementation cost in the business case.
- Updating the strategy for implementation.
- Updating the concept for benefits realisation.

Continual mobilisation of future ambassadors among managers, project managers, and change managers while handling any resistance.

Launch 2: The benefits realisation method is implemented in all projects

The change track typically includes:

- Training and change efforts for project managers and steering committees.
- Development of behavioural scripts for project managers and change managers in collaboration with them.
- Training project managers, change managers, and steering committee members to establish a shared language on benefits realisation and change, clarifying new roles and responsibilities and reducing the need for coaching and support from method specialists.

(Continued)

(*Continued*)

- Involvement of method specialists to support projects where necessary.

Other general tips

- Make it as easy as possible to attain the desired behaviour, for example by designing standard workshops, meetings, templates, and examples from several types of projects.
- Make it easy and acceptable to get help (for example from method specialists).
- Make sure that the incentive structures for both project managers and managers in the steering committees support the new ways of working.

The technical track typically includes:

- Ad hoc adjustments to project methods and tools that have been developed as part of the benefits realisation concept.

Launch 3: New PMO services are implemented

The change track typically includes:

- Anchoring of benefits realisation and change among method specialists (similar to Ørsted's internal consultants).
- Preparing a behavioural script for method specialists in collaboration with future method specialists.
- Providing coaching to method specialists until they can provide project support to benefits realisation and organisational change on their own.

(*Continued*)

(Continued)

Create demand from senior management directly and through portfolio management

- Create interest as well as demand for benefits realisation and organisational change in senior management, for example by making visible and discussing the baseline for benefits realisation and results of pilot projects.
- Drive the demand for benefits realisation and change through the portfolio's prioritisation of projects and reporting, and data requirements.

Create new behaviour for the PMO

- Develop behavioural scripts for those working in the PMO (besides the method specialists).
- Follow up on the new behaviour and adjust continually based on your organisation's feedback.

Possible strategies for implementation in your organisation

- Choose the implementation strategy that best suits your organisation and that the method specialists can support. For example, 'The largest projects first' or 'One business unit at a time'.
- Evaluate and adjust the need for ongoing support when benefits realisation is widespread throughout the organisation.

(Continued)

(Continued)

The technical track typically includes:

(Note: portfolio management and governance, capacity management, performance management, and best practice support refer to the categories of services in the benefit-driven PMO. See Figure 9.1.)

Designing the organisation's benefit-driven PMO, including the choice of services it will provide

- Adjusted processes and system support to handle portfolio management and governance.
- Adjusted processes and system support to handle capacity management expansion to include change and benefits realisation.
- Adjusting processes and system support to handle the expansion of performance management to include change and benefit data.

New processes and tools for best practice support have been created as part of launch 1 and adjusted in launch 2.

A Special Thanks to

Mads Ingemann Herskind for, after a bit of persuasion, throwing your energy and expertise in behavioural design into the work of designing our practical and benefit-driven approach to behavioural change. Your thoughts helped to lay the foundation for this book.

Helena Bjørn Bograd for always insisting that we develop and improve our methods and for your flow of good ideas as to how we achieve that. Your input has significantly improved the ways of working with benefit realisation and change. Thank you.

Jesper Krøyer Lind for the benefit realisation journey we have been on, for the days when we penned the first lines of this book and our conversations and sparring while developing our approach to benefit realisation.

I also owe a big thanks to **Thomas Gottschalck**, **Jakob Brøndsted**, and **Jesper Krøyer Lind** for being my primary review team. Thank you for sharing your specialist knowledge, your various perspectives, and your consistently honest feedback. Finally, thank you for helping me make the book clear in its purpose and language.

I would also like to thank those who have contributed content, inspiration, review, and presentation: Christian Frandsen, Christian Mark Christensen, Helene Jensen, Helle Falholt, Jesper Høi Jensen, Laust Lauridsen, Mads Lomholt, Maria Soland Berg-Nielsen, and Monique Maree Benigna. Each one of you has helped make the book everything I imagined it could be.

A SPECIAL THANKS TO

Thanks to **Nykredit**, **University of Copenhagen** and **Ørsted** for making the book practice-oriented by contributing your cases. A special thanks to **Carsten Kruse** (Nykredit), **Anders V. Møller** (formerly the University of Copenhagen), **Kenneth Theilgaard Roslind** (Ørsted), and everyone I also had the pleasure of collaborating with to create more value.

Thanks to **Jeannette Paaske Pedersen** for your great effort in translating the Danish manuscript into English. Finally, thanks to **Pernille Groth Thorsen** for volunteering to review and provide feedback for the English translation – I really appreciate it.

As a practitioner, I also owe my thanks to all the incredible people I have worked with during the past several years. And to those of you who have crossed my path at conferences, events, or courses and made me reflect on your questions and contributions. And, finally, to all of you who have shared your insights with me during casual conversations by the coffee machine. Thank you so much!

References

Axelos and Roden, E. (2013). *Portfolio, Programme and Project Offices (P3O)*. London: TSO.

Bradley, G. (2010). *Benefit Realisation Management: A Practical Guide to Achieving Benefits Through Change*. Farnham: Gower.

Budzier, A. (2014). Theorizing outliers: explaining variation in IT project performance. Thesis. Saïd Business School, University of Oxford.

Erichsen, P. (2015). Nøglen til de bedste resultater findes blandt motiverede medarbejdere. *Ledelse i Udviking* 2(April): 6–8.

Gladwell, M. (2000). *The Tipping Point: How Little Things Can Make a Big Difference*. New York: Little Brown.

Gottschalk, T., Laang, A., and Thuesen, K.B. (2017). IT projects: are our change management efforts caught in the middle? https://implementconsultinggroup.com/it-projects-are-our-change-management-efforts-caught-in-the-middle/, accessed 12 January 2022.

Grech, M., Horberry, T., and Koester, T. (2008). *Human Factors in the Maritime Domain*. Boca Raton, FL: CRC Press.

Heath, C. and Heath, D. (2007). *Made to Stick: Why Some Ideas Survive and Others Die*. London: Random House.

Herrero, L. (2011). *Homo Imitans: The Art of Social Infection: Viral Change in Action*. Beaconsfield: Meeting Minds Publishing.

Jenner, S. (2014). *Managing Benefits: Optimizing the Return from Investments*. London: TSO.

Lakoff, G. and Johnson, M. (1981). *Metaphors We Live By*. Chicago: University of Chicago.

Lampel, J., Mintzberg, H., Quinn, J.B., and Ghoshal, S. (2003). *The Strategy Process: Concepts, Contexts, Cases*. Upper Saddle River, NJ: Pearson Higher Education.

Leffingwell, D. and Jemillo, D. (2021). Safe for Lean Enterprises 5.0. https://www.scaledagileframework.com/, accessed 22 January 2022.

Loehr, J. and Schwartz, T. (2005). *The Power of Full Engagement: Managing Energy, Not Time, Is the Key to Performance and Personal Renewal*. New York: Free Press.

Maister, D., Galford, R., and Green, C. (2002). *The Trusted Advisor*. New York: Simon & Schuster.

Maurer, R. (2010). *Beyond the Wall of Resistance: Why 70% of All Changes Still Fail – and What You Can Do About It* (2nd edition). London: Bard Press.

Maurer, R. (2021). The Energy Bar. https://www.energybartools.com/resources, accessed 22 January 2022.

Maxwell, J. (2013). Overcoming resistance instead of being overwhelmed by it. https://www.johnmaxwell.com/blog/overcoming-resistance-instead-of-being-overwhelmed-by-it/, Accessed 22 January 2022.

Office of Government Commerce (2009). *Managing Successful Projects with PRINCE2*. London: TSO.

Olsson, J.R., Adland, K.T., Ehlers, M., and Ahrengot, N. (2018). *Half Double: Projects in Half the Time with Double the Impact*. Copenhagen: Implement Press.

Olsson, J.R., Ahrengot, N., and Attrup, M.L. (2019). *Power i Projekter og Porteføljer* (4th edition). Copenhagen: DJØF.

Ries, E. (2017). *The Startup Way: How Modern Companies Use Entrepreneurial Management to Transform Culture and Drive Long-Term Growth*. London: Penguin Books.

Rigsrevisionen (2020). Report on management of benefits in government it projects. https://uk.rigsrevisionen.dk/audits-reports-archive/2020/sep/report-on-management-of-benefits-in-government-it-projects, accessed 22 January 2022.

Robertson, C.T. and Kesselheim, A.S. (2018). *Blinding as a Solution to Bias: Strengthening Biomedical Science, Forensic Science, and Law*. Cambridge, MA: Academic Press.

Rock, D. (2008). SCARF: a brain-based model for collaborating with and influencing others. *NeuroLeadership Journal* 1: 1–10.

Rode, A.L.G., Hansen, A., Svejvig, P., et al. (2021). *Project Half Double: Results of Phase 1 and Phase 2*. https://ebooks.au.dk/aul/catalog/view/326/221/1000-2, accessed 22 January 2022.

Ryan, B. and Gross, N.C. (1943). The diffusion of hybrid seed corn in two Iowa communities. *Rural Sociology* 8(1): 15–24.

Rytter, R. and Jensen, J.H. (2018). Safe does not create benefits – people do. https://www.linkedin.com/pulse/safe-does-create-benefits-people-do-rasmus-rytter/, accessed 22 January 2022.

Rytter, R., Lind J.K., and Svejvig, P. (2015). *Gevinstrealisering: En praktisk guide*. Copenhagen: Akademisk Forlag.

Shaw, P. (2002). *Changing Conversations in Organizations: A Complexity Approach to Change (Complexity and Emergence in Organizations)*. London: Routledge.

Søndergaard, N.T. (2021). Short and fat projects will save your bottom line. https://implementconsultinggroup.com/article/short-and-fat-projects-will-save-your-bottom-line/, accessed 22 January 2022.

Thomas, J. and Mullaly, M. (2008). *Researching the Value of Project Management*. Pennsylvania: Project Management Institute.

Ward, J. and Daniel, E. (2012). *Benefits Management: How to Increase the Business Value of Your IT Projects*. Chichester: Wiley.

Index

Page numbers followed by *f*, *t*, and *b* refer to figures, tables, and boxes, respectively.